Effects for the Theatre

Effects for the Theatre

Editor:
GRAHAM WALNE

Contributors:
JOE AVELINE
JOHN LEONARD
GRAHAM WALNE
ESQUIRE JAUCHEM

A & C Black · London
Drama Book Publishers · New York

First published 1995
A & C Black (Publishers) Limited
35 Bedford Row, London WC1R 4JH

ISBN 0-7136-3985-7

A CIP catalogue record for this book is available from the British Library.

Published simultaneously in the USA by
Drama Book Publishers, 260 Fifth Avenue,
New York, New York 10001.

Library of Congress Cataloging-in-Publication Data
Effects for the theatre / edited by Graham Walne.
    p.   cm.
  Includes bibliographical references and index.
  Contents: Scenic effects / by Joe Aveline – Sound effects / by John Leonard – Lighting effects / by Graham Walne – Special effects / by Esquire Jauchem.
    ISBN 0-89676-136-3 : $24.95
1. Theaters – Sound effects. 2. Theaters – Lighting. 3. Theaters — Special effects.
4. Theaters – Stage-setting and scenery.
I. Walne, Graham. II. Aveline, Joe.
PN2091.S6E33 1995
792′.025–dc20
                                                94-7112
                                              CIP

Front cover photograph The Temple of Solomon burns in Verdi's *Nabucco*, New York City Opera, Effects Design, Esquire Jauchem and Gregory Meeh

Back cover photograph dry ice fog creeps through the graveyard
in the Opera Company of Boston's production of *Der Vampyr*, effects by Esquire Jauchem

Typeset in 11/12¾pt Clearface Regular by Rowland Phototypesetting Limited,
Bury St Edmunds, Suffolk.
Printed in the United Kingdom by Butler & Tanner Limited,
Frome, Somerset

Contents

Each chapter has a more detailed list of contents on the first page.

Acknowledgements

We would like to thank the following for the provision of artwork, photographs and drawings and indeed are indebted to them for their help.

Simon Ash
Joe Aveline
Lynton Black Photography
Opera Company of Boston
CCT Theatre Lighting
Phil Clifford, Royal Exchange, Manchester
David Edelstein of Triple E
Vanessa Ford Productions
David Hersey Associates (DHA)
ICI Acrylics
Esquire Jauchem
Jauchem & Meeh Special Effects, NYC
John Leonard
Gregory Meeh
Metropolitan Museum of Art
Museum of the City of New York
Northern Light
Ludwig Pani

Performing Right Society (PRS)
Richard Pilbrow
Helen Pond
Terence Rees
Richard Sound Design
Ro Theatre Rotterdam
Royal National Theatre
Royal Opera House
Rycote Windshields
Herbert Senn
Sonifex
Michael Spencer
Alan Stevenson
The Tabs Library at Strand Lighting
Triple E Group
Welsh National Opera
White Light
Graham Walne
Stephen White

Preface

I was very pleased to be asked to edit and contribute to this book which seems to fill a gap. Most effects are based on lighting, sound, mechanics or a specially created technique. Each of these areas is explored in this book by a particular expert. Joe Aveline has had a life-long interest in the history and development of stage mechanics, and is currently (among other things) Chairman of the Archaeological Committee of the Association of British Theatre Technicians. Few scenic effects rely upon a technique developed only in this century and the scenic section may help readers appreciate and utilise some of the lesser known ideas from past times, still very effective despite the apparent lack of high technology! John Leonard's work as a sound designer on both sides of the Atlantic is well known and I personally think his section on sound effects is the best currently written anywhere, notably because of the explanations of the growing digital techniques which will affect every reader within the lifetime of this book. Esquire Jauchem's name is well known in the USA and his contribution on special effects has all the hallmarks of an experienced practitioner. This section perhaps more than any other will encourage the reader to experiment safely, an essential approach because few really special effects can be bought off the shelf complete.

Some effects will appear several times in sections written by different authors and that is because the effect itself relies upon several disciplines in order to work. Fire for example involves sound, lighting and mechanical inputs; rain also can be created through the use of real water, sound or projection. The book carries cross-referencing wherever this occurs. It is the authors' hope that the book can be read either as a whole or used as a work of reference.

Inevitably, given the range and organic nature of theatre, a reader may not find in here precisely the effect he or she is looking for, but if the nature of the effect is analysed then it is the authors' belief that the book will contain a technique that will prove useful.

During the period whilst this book was being written the movie *Jurassic Park* was launched in the UK and with it, a publication on how it was made. As some readers will be aware, many of the dinosaurs were produced and operated totally through computer generated images. This film was not the first to use this technique, although it appears to have pushed the boundaries of the technique further. Such an approach is impossible for the stage effects person. Additionally another movie *The Fugitive* has recently been launched with much hype about the spectacular scene in which a real train is crashed, as far as is known, this does not use computer generated enhancement, but the real thing; however it can only be done once. Again such an approach is equally impossible for the stage effects person.

Arguably some rock concerts, grand opera and musicals, the latter notably the work of Sir Andrew Lloyd Webber, are the most spectacular stage productions of our time, but each and every one has to be capable of being repeated night after night, in some cases for many years. Not for the theatre the grand slam single once-off effect. Additionally the effect has to be tangible, there is no facility in theatre for the totally electronic effect, even sound relies on the performer and the acoustic which changes slightly night after night.

This is the essence of theatre and of its effects, communicating live and doing so in such a manner that each member of the audience, even in the knowledge that the show he or she is watching has run for years, is delivering something unique on the night they are watching.

Graham Walne

1 Introduction

WHAT IS AN EFFECT?

An effect per se, is rather difficult to define. That is to say that it may mean different things in different areas of the theatre and in different departments. A sound effect may be noise created off-stage, when we wish the audience to believe that the noise is emanating from something referred to in the action but out of view. Or it may be music underscoring the action coming from tape playback systems. Conversely one doesn't consider, for instance, the orchestra in a musical play or show to be an effect, although the same sound could be considered to be an effect if it were emerging from a mechanical reproduction system.

The same rather applies to lighting which is necessary for most performances and therefore is not an effect as such. The question is at what point does something become an effect. Could it be for instance that the setting of the sun, with shafts of light coming through a window onto a set, could be seen as an effect, or is it simply part of the realistic lighting which is taking part in this particular piece?

Whatever effect is being created, it is in fact something which has emerged from discussions between directors and designers and other senior personnel. What is seen by, or is heard by the audience, is as a result of these conversations. Whether or not it is seen as an effect as such, is perhaps less germane than the fact of a perceived need for something to happen in order to enhance the overall quality of the production. Therefore we may assume that effects are in fact led by, or directed by, directors and designers in conjunction with others who are to provide whatever the desired result might be.

HISTORY OF SCENIC EFFECTS

The history of effects in the theatre goes back an extremely long way. There is evidence that the Greeks and Romans used machines and so on to enhance their performances. Our current theatrical tradition dates back

400 years to Shakespeare and embraces the Jacobean and Caroline periods. It was during the latter periods that the idea of moving perspective sets emerged, with the wings either side being changed to give different 'pictures'. (Illustration 1.1)

1.1 Perspective
Set for the gala performance to mark the wedding of the Royal Prince of Poland, Prince Elector of Saxony.

Perspective design by Guiseppe Bibiena (1696–1756). Bibiena was one of a family of architects and designers, his father Ferdinando invented the painting of buildings viewed at an angle. It has been said that, 'These restless flights of architecture running diagonally off-stage toward undetermined distances revolutionised and dominated scenic design for most of the eighteenth century'. (A. Hyatt Mayor, Curator of Prints, Metropolitan Museum, New York.)

The scene would have been prepared using a series of cut outs with candles shining light on the one behind with the brightest lights reserved for the backdrop.

This could have been described at the time as an effect. Certainly the use of machines to lower and raise people, such as in clouds, would be considered an effect. At that time, before the invention of modern machinery and lubricants, one would imagine that these things moved in a fairly jerky way to our modern eye. However, this would not have mattered because the people at that time would not have had any greater expectation. It seems important to realise throughout any consideration of effect, this expectation level of the audience.

Over the last 400 years audience expectation has changed. One would hesitate to say it has improved, or anything which would imply that the current audience is more demanding than the one 400 years ago. For to do that one would imply that the human mind has evolved rather more than the evidence would supply. Our modern theatregoing eyes and senses totally accept the use of the lighting and sound systems as part of the normal activity involved in seeing a performance in any kind of venue.

We have become used to machinery and articles changing on the stage as though some great unseen hand were moving them from place to place, it being generally believed that this kind of thing enhances the action or delights an audience in some degree (see illustration on page 5).

Where we perhaps differ from earlier periods is that we are now enjoying the complexities of high-tech movement for their own sake rather than necessarily for the effect which they create. For instance, in the late Victorian and Edwardian times, great store was laid by spectacular disaster effects – sinking ships and submarines and airships flying off etc, which resembled to some degree the lifelike disaster, but it must be remembered that at that time there was neither cinema nor television and that the theatre wanted to mirror the reality of disaster and create an audience reaction. Nowadays with cinema and television, the theatre could not get close enough to reality to suspend the disbelief of the audience. Therefore, much of what we do nowadays on stage enters into a realm of fantasy and high technology. A similar syndrome perhaps to the remark after the invention of photography: 'After this, painting is dead'. Painters, to survive, became impressionists, surrealists etc, ie, painting what the camera could not see. This is supported by the rotating, tilting floors that you might see in West End musicals, or large mobile statues etc.

One does not expect this sort of thing to happen in everyday life. It may be, then, that the modern theatre of this high technology type, appeals to people's sense of fantasy and that people do not necessarily wish to see something which mirrors, or reminds them of, reality; in which case, if this is true, we are unlike our ancestors in Victorian times.

Throughout the history of theatre, people creating effects have used the available technology to their best abilities. What we in the theatre have always been good at is applying existing technology derived in other fields for our own purposes. The thundersheet could never have been used until the invention of strip steel mills. A similar sort of analogy would apply to almost any other effect which you see on a stage.

The Italian stage technician Niccolo Sabbatini (c.1574–1654) devised the effect of a series of waves. These were not unlike barley sugar canes ie, twisted shapes where the indentation was painted a sea-blue colour and the crests of the twists of the barley sugar were painted white. A number of these were set across the stage, each one slightly higher than the one in front. By

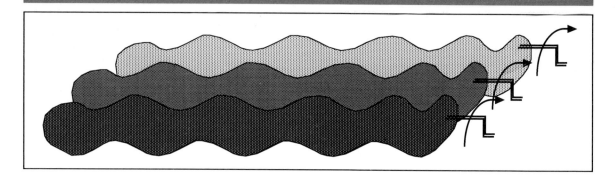

1.2 Sabbatini's Waves
The 'waves' were set at increasing heights above the stage floor and were rotated via the handles positioned at either end. This creates an undulating surface as viewed from the auditorium. The raised parts of the waves were frequently painted white, or even textured before painting, giving the impression of rolling sea.

rotating these, using the handles at each end, the impression given was of undulating waves. (Illustration 1.2)

It was possible for performers or pieces of scenery to be seen swimming through, sinking into or rising from the waves. There were ample opportunities for their use in the Baroque opera. There is a complete installation of these in the Drottningholm Theatre, Sweden. (This eighteenth century theatre remained closed for over 100 years, then was rediscovered and reopened in 1921 with its original fittings intact.) These waves were not Sabbatini's only piece of magic. In 1638, Sabbatini had published a handbook for making scenery and effects, *Practica di Fabricar Scene é Machine ne Teatri*, which contained many more magical effects.

Since then, other systems for producing wave effects have been used. At the end of the last century in the Theatre Royal, Drury Lane, ships subsided beneath cutout waves. In more modern times companies use rolls of silk stretched across the stage and fluttered from both sides giving the effect of the rising and falling of movement of the sea.

HISTORY OF SOUND EFFECTS

Sound effects and music have long played an important part in drama. The Greeks used music and the recreation of natural sounds by the chorus to aid the telling of the story and much medieval drama is full of sound and fury. Shakespeare wrote many sound effects into his plays, mostly battle and storm noises that could be recreated with ease by the use of percussion instruments or simple effects devices. Where he needed spectacle on a grand scale, music and sound effects were used together and, at a performance of *Henry VIII* at the Globe Theatre in 1613, a reporter noted the disastrous effect an over-enthusiastic effects operator can have on a production!

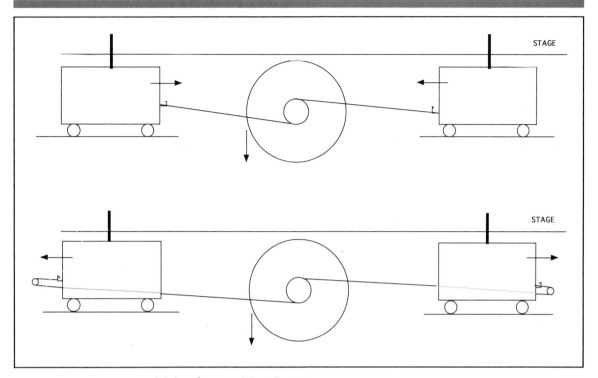

1.3 Synchronous Wing System

This system was developed in Italy in the seventeenth century and became the most common form of moving pieces of scenery in continental theatre for 200 years. Using this device entire sets could be changed in unison by crew operating the drum drive system.

The diagram shows how winged flats could be pulled both on and off stage by being hooked to the drum and shaft (the circles in the middle) below the stage. The rectangles represent substage frames which roll back and forth on rails. The dark line represents a pole which projects above the level of the stage with the scenery attached. The diagram shows scenery being moved on stage, and off stage by use of pulleys, separately, but in fact as many as ten or twelve frames could be moved on and off stage at the same time. Lines were switched around so that scenery could be pulled off stage or on as necessary. Some installations used a capstan as the drive system.

'Now to let matters of state sleep. I will entertain you at the present with what hath happened at the Bankside. The King's Players had a new play representing some principal pieces of the Reign of Henry the 8th which was set forth with many extraordinary circumstances of Pomp and Majesty . . . Now, certain canons being shot off, some of the Paper or other stuff where with some of them were stopped, did light on the Thatch, where being thought at first but an idle smoak, and their eyes more attentive to the show, it kindled inwardly and ran round like a train, consuming the whole House to the very ground . . . Only one man had his breeches set on fire, that would have perhaps have broyled him if he had not by the benefit of provident wit put it out with bottle ale.'

Shakespeare was also a realist – where sound effects were impossible to recreate, the actors simply told the audience what was going on. The more bizarre effects preceding the assassination of Julius Caesar are reported by the actors and the actual sounds themselves are left to the best effects generator, the audience's own imagination.

'The noise of battle hurtled in the air,
Horses did neigh, and dying men did groan,
and ghosts did shriek and squeal about the streets'

Shakespeare sticks to simpler effects such as thunder and lets his text do the rest. Similarly in *Henry V*, the prelude to the Battle of Agincourt is described by the Prologue, beginning with the words,

'Now entertain conjecture of a time,
When creeping murmur and the poring dark,
Fills the wide vessel of the universe.
From camp to camp through the foul womb of night,
The hum of either army stilly sounds,
That the fixed sentinels almost receive
The secret whispers of each other's watch:
Fire answers fire, and through their paly flames
Each battle sees the others umbered face:
Steed threatens steed, in high and boastful neighs
Piercing the night's dull ear, and from the tents
The armourers, accomplishing the knights,
With busy hammers closing rivets up,
Give dreadful note of preparation:
The country cocks do crow, the clocks do toll
And the third hour of drowsy morning name.'

With descriptive writing of that order, who needs sound effects? When producing Shakespeare plays today it is very tempting to embellish the textual references with unnecessary sounds and, unless the production style calls for it, such temptation is best avoided.

In complete contrast, the Victorian theatre was obsessed with special effects. Much of the stage machinery that we take for granted today, developed and perfected during the Victorian era, is described in Chapter 2. Mechanical sound effects machines were built to simulate the sounds of weather, transport and disasters, both natural and unnatural. Such machines were the province of the property master and in some theatres, until recently, mechanical effects such as door slams were still handled by the props department, rather than the sound department. Such mechanical devices still have their place in modern theatre and should be investigated in circumstances where modern techniques fail to provide a satisfactory alternative. A comprehensive list of sound effects and their mechanical means of production can be found in the excellent book *Sound in the Theatre*, by Harold Burris-Meyer, Vincent Mallory and Lewis S. Goodfriend.

In the early part of the twentieth century two plays were produced in Britain that required exceedingly complicated sound effects plots: *The Ghost Train* by Arnold Ridley and *Journey's End* by R. C. Sherriff. The effects plots for these two plays make fascinating reading. It is worth noting that more people are needed off-stage to operate the effects for *The Ghost Train* than are needed on stage to perform the play.

Effects were still being reproduced mechanically in the mid 1920s and it was not until the introduction of electronic amplification and recording systems, spurred on by the widespread use of sound in cinema, that techniques changed. The ability to record sounds, whether created naturally or artificially, and then to replay them accurately night after night changed the way that sound effects in theatre were used. The production of effects was no longer the responsibility of the property man; a specialist, skilled in the mysteries of electronics, would be required to negotiate the new, complex machinery of disc player, amplifier and loudspeaker. A new opportunity for accuracy and creativity was introduced: loudspeakers could be placed at strategic locations on a set or in the auditorium to give the required directional information, and portable recording equipment, at first on disc recorders and later on tape recorders, meant that sounds could be recorded on location for later playback in the theatre.

In the late 1940s the magnetic tape recorder became freely available as a tool for use in film and broadcast, but theatre performance requirements dictated a system of replay that was repeatable, easy to locate and accurate to cue, and so the Panatrope was devised. The Panatrope was a console with two or more disc players with cueing devices on the pick-up arms and a level control for each output. Switching for various speakers could also be provided so that the operator could send a particular effect to the relevant speaker with the minimum possible fuss. Specialists companies existed to supply theatres with the sound effects that they needed per production: a list was prepared and dispatched to the sound library who would prepare a special set of gramophone records for each cue in the show. The operator would then place each disc on the turntable, position the pick-up arm precisely over the start of the track, and then lower the arm and increase the output of the player to the desired level. Multiple cues relied on a great deal of manual dexterity on behalf of the operator and the fairly coarse quality of the stylus meant that disks wore out after a number of performances and had to be replaced. Considering how fraught with danger the entire operation was, it is surprising that it took so long for the use of disks to disappear from theatre sound. The arrival of the compact magnetic tape recorders in the late 1950s made the life of the theatre sound man much easier and is a method of effects reproduction still in use in the majority of theatres at the time of writing.

Digital audio, familiar to most people in the form of domestic replay media such as Compact Disc, Digital Compact Cassette, Mini Disc, and

Digital Audio Tape, is making great changes in the way that we think of using sound effects in the theatre and the many and various options open to the sound man or woman in theatre today is discussed in Chapter Three.

HISTORY OF LIGHTING EFFECTS

Perhaps the earliest lighting effect was the oil lantern used by the Ancient Greeks to denote that night had fallen, a useful cue since the performances took place in the afternoon sun! This is worthy of note today since many productions cannot afford, or choose to avoid, the use of realistic scenery and a practical light fitting, candle or simulated oil lamp can bring an instant sense of period and time to an otherwise bare stage whilst providing motivation for the lighting design.

As the theatre moved indoors then stage lighting for illumination purposes developed and we will exclude that from this overview and concentrate on the pure effect. However it must be said that the early stage lighting engineers and designers, notably those of Italy in the sixteenth century (see Sabbatini on pages 3–4), must have created many effects through their experimentation with lenses and silk colour filters. Later in the early nineteenth century when the gasplate enabled central control over dimming to take place, the very action of a co-ordinated fade or cross-fade became an effect in itself and the use of gauze to cause appearances and disappearances dates from the development of gas controls.

By the seventeenth century the ability to sink the footlights below the stage, and to physically swivel the lights so that they shine into the wings away from the action, all enhanced the use of sunrise, sunset and moon effects. By the eighteenth century designers had become virtual household names as they added fog and fire to their repertoire, these effects being enhanced in the nineteenth century by the arrival of gas and its naked flame, typical is the use of gas fires behind asbestos coal. It is this era which saw the development of lycopodium and magnesium powder to create flashes. Not surprisingly many theatres suffered serious fires and it was partially this which led Richard Wagner to replace the more dangerous substances with steam.

At this point the magic lantern makes its appearance in entertainment (although in existence many years earlier) as a sophisticated slide projector in which the action of cross-fading between synchronised images created dissolving continuous scenes, many containing movement through mechanical adjustment within the slide itself. The first recorded use of this device in the theatre was in Kean's performance as King Lear at Drury Lane in 1820 in which it was used to project 'supernatural' colours and patterns on Lear himself. Later in 1927 the magic lantern was used to project scenery in *The Flying Dutchman*. Many productions used the lantern to project ghosts and apparitions.

The development in 1816 of the limelight, originally used in surveying and then borrowed by the theatre as a followspot (initially from the wings and flies rather than from the auditorium), provided the theatre with its most intense source of light to date and thus it became used to represent moon and sun beams. It is worth noting that towards the end of the nineteenth century the larger theatres would employ up to 30 limelights in each production.

A seminal lighting effect was created in 1883 for the finale of Gilbert and Sullivan's *Iolanthe* in which the fairies carried a cell which stored electricity and enabled them to dance with illuminated stars in their hair, hence the expression 'fairy light'.

The early development of electric light is marked by many notable engineers and designers, especially David Belasco, whose use of early spotlights and reflected light to simulate sunset and sunrise partially stimulated Puccini to write the opera *Madama Butterfly* based upon the play he had just witnessed.

Of the many influential people in the twentieth century Adolph Linnebach is notable for the system of shadow projection which he developed in 1916 and which now bears his name, effectively the only form of theatre projection (excluding the overhead projectors used in lecture theatres) in which the slide can be made up in situ and the effect judged instantly. Adrian Samoiloff also gave his name to the effect of the use of complementary colours to change colours present in costumes or scenery, suits would change into pyjamas and girl dancers gain or lose clothing. It is reported that artists were provided with dressing room make-up lighting to match that on the stage so that they could adjust their make-up appropriately. It was obviously worth the expense since apparently the response at the box-office matched the interest shown in the effect by the newspapers of the time (1924).

Readers who wish to learn more of the history of stage lighting are directed to what is generally regarded as the bible, Terence Rees *Theatre Lighting in the Age of Gas* published in 1978 by the Society for Theatre Research. The book also contains reference to other complementary aspects of lighting effects such as the use of gauze, traps, and explosions.

2 Scenic and Mechanical Effects JOE AVELINE

PREPARING AND INTERFACING

As an example of how multi-disciplinary an effect can become, I propose to look at one specific example in some detail so that the broader picture can be seen.

Gauze can be used to create the effect of initially disclosing something and then obscuring it, and vice-versa, sometimes referred to as a dissolve. This is done by altering the lighting state so that when the gauze is lit from the front, you see the gauze material itself or what is painted upon it (as an opaque or semi-opaque surface) and when it is lit from behind, you see those objects which have been placed behind the gauze, through the gauze.

The gauze dissolve is what can be accurately described as an effect, but, as with most effects, its success depends on a large degree of co-operation from a large number of disciplines, especially scenery and lighting. Every individual involved must bring to the discussion table their expertise and their considered opinions as to the viability of what their department can offer towards the success of the whole.

The scenic design has to be carefully scrutinised in order to make the first decision and that is to choose the colour of the gauze. The normal gauzes used for scenery are available in white, grey or black and it is important to discuss which one of these would be the best for the particular circumstances, depending on the colour and density of the design.

Another factor to consider is that there are commonly two types of gauze to choose from: scenic gauze and sharkstooth gauze (see illustration 2.1). The sharkstooth gauze has much smaller apertures than the scenic gauze and can accept the paint better and provide a more opaque surface. Sharkstooth gauze is better for large pictorial representations and because of its density tends to be preferred for dissolves. Scenic gauze which, with its larger holes, tends to take paint less well is often employed unpainted to fog the whole stage picture if placed downstage or to diffuse the cyc if placed

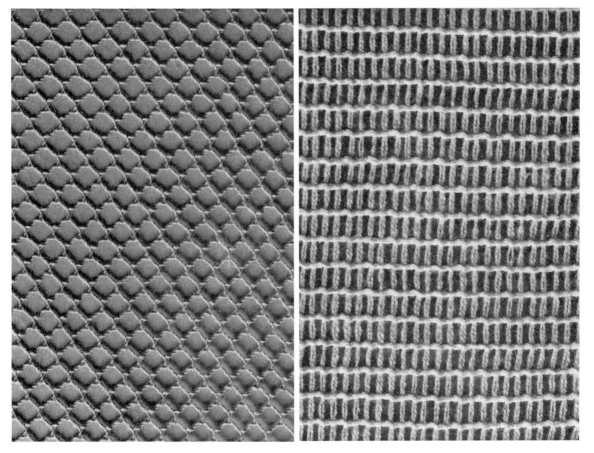

2.1 Gauzes
These two pictures show two commonly used types of gauze. The more open weave scenic gauze (left) can almost invariably be seen through as it offers a minimal surface for the application of paint. In black and untreated, it can almost disappear.

The closer woven sharkstooth gauze (right) can, correctly handled, be made virtually opaque.

Both pictures are larger than life so that the weave details can be seen more easily.

upstage (see **Gauze** page 15). The required quality of vision through the gauze must be taken into account. This point particularly concerns painters who must be aware of what the effect is when they apply paint, and make sure that all the holes in the gauze are open; thus thinner paint will attract less light and thicker paint more, etc. Dyes are also used.

Another consideration is the context of the performance ie, the dissolve effect must be seen in relation to what preceeds and follows it. The duration of the effect also has a relationship with the degree of credibility of the effect itself. The siting of the gauze on stage relative to what is set behind, it has to inform the next part of the process. The light hitting the face of the gauze, illuminating the front and giving the impression of opacity, will also, in part, pass through the gauze and illuminate things which are behind, if they are set in close proximity. They will then be visible when they should not be. The lighting designer should have a view here as to the practicality of what is being proposed insofar that he or she has to provide a wash of light of some intensity in order to render the surface face of the gauze opaque. It is important that the gauze is situated in a position on stage where it can be suitably lit. The thinner the gauze itself, or the thinner the painting on it, the more acute the lighting angle will need to be to achieve opacity. The gauze needs to be hung or stretched avoiding creases which spoil the final effect.

If it is necessary or desirable to obscure what is behind, then articles set upstage must be far enough away and out of the angle of the light that is hitting the front. And the light, which is to illuminate the articles behind, must emerge from light sources which are set on the far side of the gauze from which the audience is seeing it. It is also quite common for opaque cloths or tabs to be set immediately upstage of a gauze to obscure the scene to be revealed, and that these are then taken out a few seconds before the lighting starts to change to effect the 'bleed' through the gauze.

To summarise, the following points should be considered when creating a dissolve effect: location of gauze in relation to what will be revealed behind it, location of gauze in relation to lighting equipment, space behind gauze for scenery and lighting, and the pictorial representation required on the gauze. These points should be considered along with the type, colour and expense of the gauze. Incorrect choice of a gauze can spoil the desired effect.

Once these decisions have been made the people concerned with the staging should be informed. For example, a character blocked to stand just upstage of the gauze whilst the gauze is being lit from the front, will certainly be seen through it and the director must be told that this is not a good place for them to be, if the effect is to be maintained.

It is clear then that the simple words 'let us do a dissolve here', involves a lot of considered thought from a number of different departments in order for it to be brought successfully to a conclusion.

OVERVIEW

Scenic and mechanical effects are the parents, as it were, of all other theatrical effects besides those created by the performers. If one accepts the concept of 'theatre' for our purposes as being a performance played on some kind of stage, or something representing a stage, then almost invariably scenery or other devices are used to give the impression of this stage having a certain shape or picture which conforms to the needs of the particular play. Perhaps the use of the word 'parents' is a bit pejorative because it was only circumstance which created the situation. In the Classical theatre, played outdoors, the only lighting effect would have been provided by the gods and so beyond the scope of mere mortals.

Scenic and mechanical effects can be broken down into further sections:

SCENIC EFFECTS

The purpose of this section, is to look at the effects created by the use of scenery which is not moving or does not have to move for the effect to be created.

The most common form of scenic effect is the painted effect. The use of paint in the theatre dates back to the Greek theatre in the fourth century BC, where there are references to painting being used in the play *Aescylus*. The Greek word for scene painting was 'skenography', which is similar to the commonly used word 'scenographer' which means 'designer of scenery'.

The Romans, utilising some Greek ideas produced, by the beginning of the Empire, a generic theatre building which survived until the fourth century AD. So it was nearly 2000 years ago that Vitruvius, in his treatise on the design and building of theatres, referred to three kinds of scenery (painting) being used: *tragic*, where the painting delineated columns, pediments and other things suitable to kings; *comic*, where the painting was of private dwellings, balconies, and so on; and *satyric*, where trees, cabins, mountains and other mystic objects are delineated in a landscape style. Therefore, from an early beginning, the use of visual painted imagery was deemed essential for the creation of a theatrical effect.

Years later, at the beginning of the Renaissance period in Italy, Vitruvius' treatise was translated and published, inspiring the design of many theatres. His work enabled Palladio to build the Teatro Olimpico at Vicenza, completed in 1584. Although Roman in style this theatre does incorporate a perspective set which is a solid built structure. However, very shortly afterwards, at the beginning of the seventeenth century came the invention of wings, or canvas covered flats, which when painted would give a perspective effect. The use of such painted wings was to be a prime force of theatrical effect for a period of nearly 250 years.

Painting is not a skill which can be easily acquired and scene painters of calibre are worth their weight in gold and tend to improve with experience. It is apparent that scenic painting will remain, for the foreseeable future, one of the greatest sources of theatrical effect.

The use of painting for an effect in the theatre has continued through the centuries as theatres became larger and the designs evolved. New materials have been developed both for painting with and for painting on. Despite what the eye might at first discern there is rarely anything on stage which has not been altered in appearance by the addition of some compound or other by one of the accepted methods of painting. This applies not only to scenery but also to costumes and properties.

As developments in lighting have produced brighter, more intense light and colour, scenic designers and painters are obliged to produce work which bears ever closer scrutiny.

Until the twentieth century most of the traditional scene painting would have been of a figurative nature ie, the depiction of some kind of understood reality. (See colour illustration 1) Contemporary designers (see page 3) are often less interested in figurative reality and many explore the stage as a space using more abstract shapes with less precise painting requirements. This is not to say that the traditional skills are no longer needed, they are, especially where they are applied to architectural perspective, in a technique called *trompe l'oeil*, literally to trick the eye. There are a number of other common techniques which should be noted.

This seems an appropriate point to take note of the words of Lesley Woolnough, currently the doyenne of English scenic artists. Writing in 1981 she said 'strangely enough even solid moulding (as opposed to traditional flat painted ones) seemed to require strengthening by painting because the stage lighting is probably for effect and not just to simulate an ordinary source of light. Thus the stage lighting often has a "flattening" effect on solid mouldings'.

Further, 'the business of getting colour right on the job owes much to the work by the Impressionists on light, such as that colour match obtained by imperceptible spattering instead of the tedious matching of paper samples. Colour "in the big" looks different from the model, even if the colour match is spot on. In any event a broken lay in is much more interesting than flat colour and very much more lively.'

Ms Woolnough's philosophy remains timeless advice for the scenic effect painter. 'In the final analysis the essential ingredients of successful scene painting must surely be the enjoyment, the sensual delight of painting and movement.'

It is beyond the scope of a volume such as this to offer comprehensive instructions on a 400 year old art form but we may note different applications of painting beyond the creation of the immediate stage picture.

Back painting

This refers to painting the rear, unseen, side of a cloth or scenic material. This is done when the cloth is to be lit from the rear as well as the front. Back painting selected areas will prevent the light coming through to the front. At the same time the back areas not painted will appear to glow. This can be used for a wide variety of applications, eg, windows, sunsets, distant fire and so on. Naturally the thinner the material the more light will come through. It is essential to do the figurative painting on the visible surface first and that it be thoroughly dry before applying back paint otherwise there is a danger of the back paint coming through the material and spoiling the effect. The best colour for back paint is a sort of tidal sludge or river (eg, Thames) mud! This offers adequate opacity and rarely affects the tone of the front surface. If seamed cloths are to be used, designers need to be careful and keep the translucent parts of the cloth between the seams in order to avoid a series of nasty black seam shadow lines. To enhance the translucent effect, especially for windows, the window apertures may be cut out once the cloth has been painted. Then muslin or calico may be pasted on the back face allowing light to be seen in the windows from the front. If the proposed light levels are likely to be very high, painting alone may not suffice and another layer of material may have to be applied. There is a functional use for back painting where lighting instruments themselves shine through to the front of fabric scenery; the unwanted light can be minimised by painting the offending area from behind.

Breaking down or distressing

This refers to the process of distorting the appearance of an article to make it look aged, weathered, dirty, wet or whatever. Typical are the grease stains found around the kitchen sink. Experiments should be done before the main task is undertaken. Sprays, rags, knives and brushes can all be used to apply paints, bleaches and other chemicals. Anyone undertaking breaking down should have a clear image of what the final finish will be.

The same expression is used to describe the process of making things non-reflective or dulling down a pale flat or tablecloth which is catching the light too much. Conversely real objects can be enhanced by a similar application of paint, for example, into the folds and fullness of drapes as they hang.

Ultraviolet paint

Ultraviolet paint is only really used when there is to be an effect created in a blackout. Because it is reacting to the ultraviolet light, it is important that no other finish is applied over the top of the ultraviolet paint. In addition, because this effect is being carried out in conjunction with the lighting department, it is wise to experiment before commencing the main work. Ultraviolet paint is available in powder form which may be mixed with either water-soluable or other media before application. Luminous paints also shine in the dark provided they have been exposed to light beforehand.

Texturing

A thick mixture which dries in shapes left by the process of application. All manner of materials can be used in the mixture: size, sawdust, plaster emulsion paint, papier-mâché, resin filler and so on. It is best to experiment before the final application. The use of texture softens sharp edges, provides the basis for brick or stone work and gives an interesting surface to light.

Gauze

Gauze can be used to enhance the effect of infinite horizon, it is common to put one in front of a cyclorama to give a slight hazing effect. A frequently used and successful material for skies and horizons is yet another type of gauze known as 'filled gauze' which is based on a sharkstooth (see page 11) with the holes filled in with more woven material. The advantage of this is that it provides very low levels of reflection and absorbs lots of light and therefore gives the impression of great depth where there is in fact none. It is also easy to stretch into a crease-free surface.

If one simply wants to have a black surface through which one sees something behind when the lights change, again, this is a fairly simple undertaking and black is certainly the best colour gauze to use, but there are other factors to consider (see **Preparing and Interfacing** on pages 10–12). And again, if the scene before the light change is short, scenic gauze can be quite effective. It must be obvious that with scenic gauze the lighting angle needs to be more acute to the gauze in order that the light picks up as much as possible of the weave to render it to some degree opaque.

Moiré effect

Gauzes can be used to create their own effects. If two gauzes are placed one in front of the other – naturally both being stretched out – and one is moved, a moiré effect is created, not dissimilar to the sheen of watered silk or the shimmer of a water mirage. Different effects can be created by either using two similar gauzes or by combining sharkstooth and scenic gauzes.

Man-made materials

The proliferation of manufacturers of plastic products has led to the invention of plastic materials which are as effective as mirrors and other reflective surfaces. People have used effects incorporating the use of plastic mirror material where the mirroring of a reflective substance is not fully applied ie, that it is only half or one-third silver coated. The plastic mirror material can be used to produce the same effects as gauze, the effect is somewhat hazier but can be very effective within the right context.

The general advance in plastics has also produced a wide range of vacuum formed shapes and mouldings which can be attached to scenic surfaces. They save time and are lightweight; nevertheless they still require painting. On no account should any plastic be used without regard to fire regulations.

MECHANICAL EFFECTS

For the purposes of this section on mechanical effects, it is assumed that an effect is something which is moved in front of the audience during the course of the action of a performance. This is to separate it from the changing of scenery out of view of the audience, or the various different types of technique and/or use of material that is sometimes used to create scenic effects of a static pictorial nature.

For the purposes of describing these effects, it is more sensible to discuss the various different types of movement which are available rather than to discuss specific effects themselves. The following sections refer specifically then to lateral movement and vertical movement.

Vertical movement

Ever since people started to build theatres there has been vertical movement. The eighteenth century theatre-goer was frequently offered the vision of clouds replete with 'gods' flying across or descending to the stage itself. Until the latter half of the nineteenth century theatres were made of wooden frames, which limited the size and height of the structures, so they tended to have rather low grids compared to present-day practice. The advent of steel and structured concrete has allowed the construction of ever higher suspension locations above the stage. The high grid simplifies the flying in and out of large backcloths which previously had to be tripped or tumbled.

In modern theatres vertical movement is usually achieved by means of a system of counter-weights, which allows objects to be raised and lowered with relative ease by one individual who is able to control the speed and define the point of stop travelling in either direction. For effect purposes, speed is usually quite critical, especially if the piece is being flown in sight of the audience during the currency of music. Hydraulically powered systems are also becoming popular.

Tumbling

This is where the flown or suspended object is made of soft material and has a pole attached to the bottom round which it can wind itself. By winding or pulling ropes or cords in the opposite direction to the cloth, by pulling or releasing them, the cloth can be wound up and down. This is naturally an effective way of bringing something in or out of view when there is

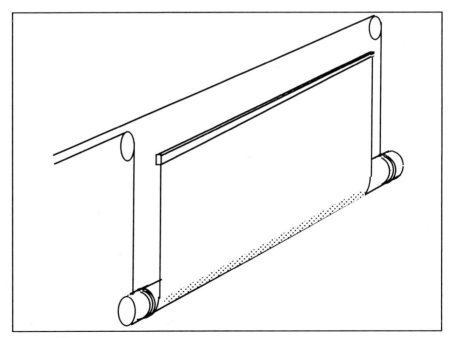

2.2 Tumble
The cloth rolls itself up as the lines round the pole are pulled. This device is useful where no flying height is available.

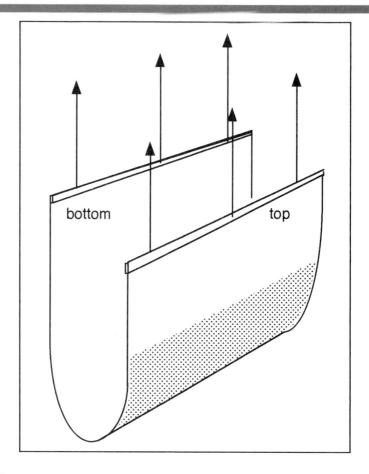

2.3 Trip
The lines attached to the bottom of the cloth enable it to be folded in two, thereby reducing the height required to pull it out of view. In very restricted situations, further flying lines can be attached to a batten along the middle of the cloth from behind reducing the height further.

restricted headroom as it does not require the top of the object to move in order to roll it in or out of sight. (See illustration 2.2 on page 17)

Tripping

This is a kind of hybrid where, with restricted height, the whole of the suspended item is raised for about half its height and then with an additional set of lines the bottom can be pulled out of the way, therefore folding it in half. (Illustration 2.3)

Lifts, traps, bridges and sloats

Until the present century a lot of emphasis was put on moving things vertically from the space below stage. In fact, it was as though the stage was a kind of halfway house between the machinery below and the machinery above so that things could be brought to the acting area from either of those two directions. The substage area developed into a maze of timberwork

2.4 Lifts

Scissor – a motor drives a screw thread which moves one pair of 'legs' closer to the other fixed pair thus forcing the platform to be raised, and vice-versa.

Chain – hauled up and down by industrial chains on linked sprockets.

Screw Jack – driven up and down by threads powered through synchronised gearboxes, the left-hand drawing shows the drives outside the lift, the right-hand drawing shows the drives under the lift platform and sinking into wells provided below.

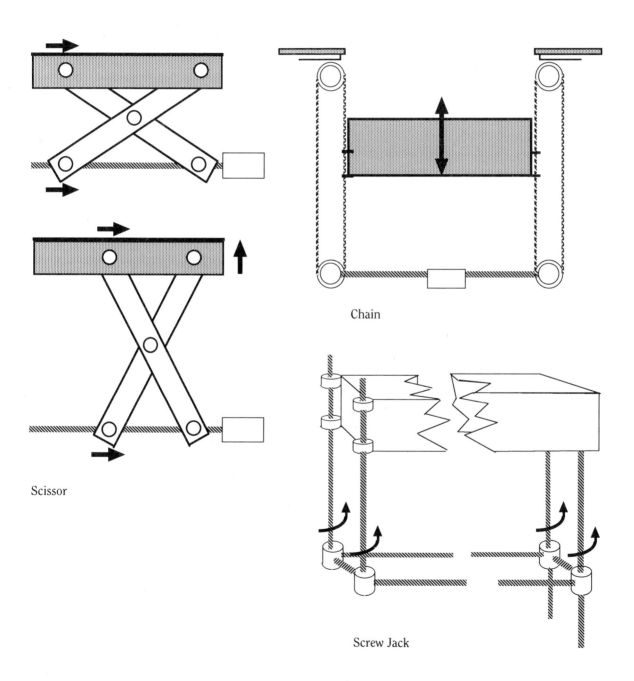

Chain

Scissor

Screw Jack

where sometimes many operators were required. These machines broadly break down into the following categories: lifts, traps, bridges and sloats. They remain part of the standard kit of stage machinery.

The word trap usually refers to a square opening in the stage floor provided with a raise and lower mechanism whereby a performer can be brought to the stage from below or the vice-versa. Some installations have considerable travel below stage and can generate enough speed to project the performer up into the air. Many theatres still have traps which are normally located either side downstage. The systems consist of a solid rostrum-like frame, on which the performer stands, set in rails or guides. The simplest traps have ropes leading to weights on two sides and rely on muscle-power to activate the required movement.

Lift, within the context of stage terms, usually means a large area which is equipped with a raise and lower facility. One of the commonest examples being the orchestra lift which can become a forestage one day, have two rows of seats the next and descend further to accommodate the musicians on the third.

In earlier times bridges were long lifts which laterally spanned the stage. The word now refers to walkways suspended at height across the stage which may or may not be connected to a motorised winch. They are frequently used for lighting equipment enabling staff to reach the instruments without the aid of ladders.

Sloats are slots in the stage into which flat scenic pieces can be set and raised into view. They are useful for obscuring other activity upstage which can then be revealed by lowering the sloat. Sloats are not currently in vogue. However, highly effective use of sloats is included in the current London production of *Phantom of the Opera*. Groundrows can be used to create the effect of a deep cavern – the largest being positioned in sloats downstage, gradually reducing in height towards the back of the stage.

Festoons or reefs   These are curtains which have rows of rings sewn on the back with pulling cords passing through them. As the cords are pulled the drapes furl up from the bottom. Festoons have the advantage of being self-contained and can thus be built into a piece of scenery and move about with it. (See illustration 2.5)

Tableaux and swags   Similar to festoons except that the rings are sewn into a diagonal line which produces the traditional stage opening shape. The great advantage of this system is that the stage picture opens and closes from a point in the middle and, subtly used, can add meaning to the beginnings and ends of scenes. A dynamic effect is produced if the curtain is flown whilst being simultaneously swagged because the resultant movement is then along the diagonal rather than the more usual horizontal or vertical. The disadvantage is that over a period of time the material 'wears' along the line of the rings because of the weight of fabric rubbing along itself. Additionally when fully drawn up the material occupies a substantial space and this can prevent flying from taking place immediately upstage of the tab. (See illustration 2.6 on page 22)

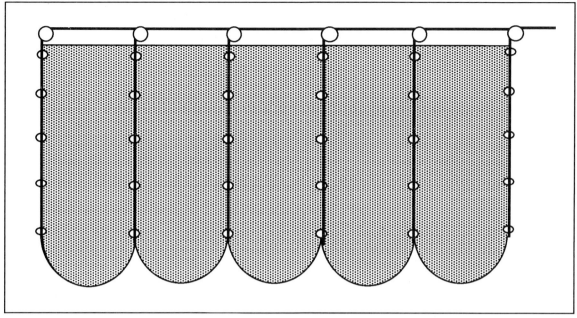

2.5 Festoon Curtain
Lines are threaded through the rings which are sewn on the back of the fabric. When the lines are operated in synchronisation it will create the festoon effect. This type of curtain is also known as the 'reefer'. If the lines are not operated in synchronisation, but pulled into a pattern then the lower edge of the curtain will assume a shape, this type of curtain is known as a 'contour' curtain.

Flying people

The mechanics of the most commonly used people-flying mechanisms are, in fact, extremely simple. The implications for safety and planning are considerably less simple. Firstly, the individual to be flown has to be securely fitted and arranged into a harness which is capable of taking their weight, without causing the individual undue discomfort, and which still enables them to move their limbs and breathe and therefore act, whilst the flying operation is going on. Usually the point of connection is a hook behind the upper back and lower neck.

Someone picked up at this point will tend to hang almost vertically with a very small lean forward. If a larger lean forward is required, then obviously, the hook for the pick up may be moved further down the back between the shoulder blades, thereby affecting the body's centre of gravity in relation to the hanging wire.

It is usual for each individual to be controlled by a special off-stage operator. The impression of flying is created by the combination of the lift given by the off-stage operator and the directional impetus given by the artiste. For example, a person simply picked up from a vertical wire will not appear to fly in any direction at all; for this directional flying to be successfully achieved, it is essential that the person being flown stands some

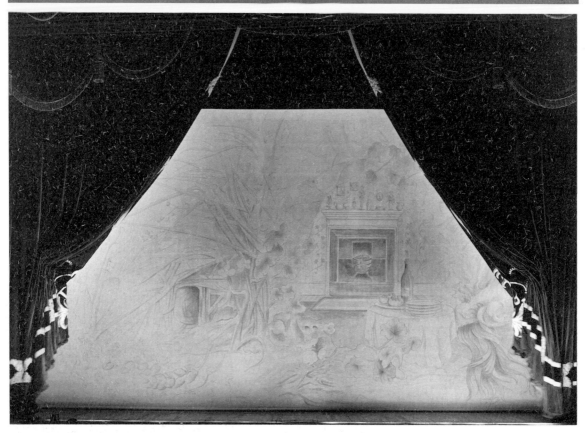

2.6 Opening Tabs
The house curtains at the Royal Opera House 'swagging' out to open the Beatrix Potter ballet. The draw lines behind the drape run through a series of rings sewn onto the lining of the drape itself. This most traditional method of opening the tabs is also the simplest. The tops of the tabs can be fixed in one place which doesn't have to move. This system was after all designed for theatres before the advent of high grids and fly towers.

distance away from the location of their suspension device. As they are lifted they will start to swing towards it and this, accompanied with appropriate actions, can give the impression of flying. Naturally, if the artiste is experienced, they may also push themselves off as they are lifted and propel themselves laterally towards a destination. Their arrival there will be aided by the person off-stage operating the device and ensuring that they drop on the landing spot when they get there. Great co-ordination in this instance is required. There are firms that specialise in this sort of mechanism, and it is not recommended that people undertake to do it with home-made bits of kit which could prove to be a danger to the artiste and any others who may be standing around. (See illustration on page 23)

There are also specialists who can provide equipment to move artistes laterally as well as vertically to give an even more sophisticated impression of flying, including being able to rotate the artiste whilst the artiste is

2.7 Drum and Shaft
Drum and shaft as installed (1906) at the Playhouse Theatre, London. The most common form of gearing in the theatre for over 100 years. The load is applied to the narrow diameter of the shaft. It is moved by hauling on the line around the larger drum. The reduction of the load is proportionate to the difference between the larger and smaller diameters.

One advantage of this system is synchronous movement. A number of separate units can be attached to the shaft with the certainty that they will all start, stop and move in total unison.

A derivative of this system is used for controlling the flying of people.

airborne. As before, it cannot be recommended that individuals try to undertake these effects without competent professional assistance and equipment.

The harnesses used for flying are also similar to the ones used for simulating 'sudden drops', eg, hanging. This is an even more dangerous exercise and yet is required in a number of plays. It is obvious that the harness and the suspension fitted to the harness do actually take the artiste's weight as well as whatever additional sudden jerk strain that may be generated by a 'sudden drop'. The simulated 'hanging' rope should be slack at all times. It is most important that, when any exercise of this nature is being undertaken, the artiste is kept in consistent consultation and that they are comfortably fitted into the harness such that it will not chafe or rub their skin, causing painful damage. Badly adjusted harnesses can also have the effect of restricting the artiste's air supply, thereby not only affecting their ability to act or sing, but also their very physical integrity. One has experienced artistes who, in the interests of 'getting their show on', sometimes do not raise problems at the fitting stage, only to find that there are problems at a less apt time in the production cycle. The artiste must, therefore, be encouraged to voice any concerns or worries before they become critical.

Lateral movement

Lateral movement has been the commonest form of creating scenic effect or change in modern theatre. Laying aside the perspective wing flats, the present theatre relies enormously on things moving across the stage surface from one place to another. However, lateral movement can also take place above the stage.

Tracks

This is most commonly effected by the use of curtain tracks or tab tracks. Most people will be familiar with the standard draw curtains which act as front curtains for a lot of smaller stage installations. However, the basic track along which the curtain runs is capable of a wide variety of applications. Not only may the curtains draw on or off the stage, tracks may also carry items of scenery or flats across to form different design shapes and there is nothing whatsoever to stop one setting the track at an angle which is not necessarily parallel to the front of the stage.

The track must be considered as though it were some kind of theatrical meccano. The track itself is standard, it being no more than a rail for things to run on. It is how one applies the various different pulleys and pieces to it which enables the track to carry out the function that is desired. Some tracks can be converted to the use of linear motors whereby the traditional cord by which one pulls the drape or whatever is suspended on the track is

2.8 (Top right) The drawing shows how track systems are made up from a number of stock parts assembled to suit any particular application. Tracks are by no means a new way of achieving movement and components exist for most modes of use. It is advisable to contact a hire company or manufacturer before rejecting any design idea no matter how far fetched it may initially appear.

2.9 Linear Track Motor (Bottom right)
The motor takes the place of the lead bobbin in rope or wire hauled systems. The motor pulls itself along the track by use of magnetic fields. When linear motors were first invented it was considered that they would be a suitable motive force for high speed railways. This theatrical application of the principle allows the mechanical hauling line to be dispensed with. This is especially useful when the track describes curves or corners which require complex diverter pulleys if hauling lines are in use. The system is based on standard track with conductor rails bolted on, which supply current and instructions to the motor. It is also possible to use more than one unit on the same track giving greater design flexibility.

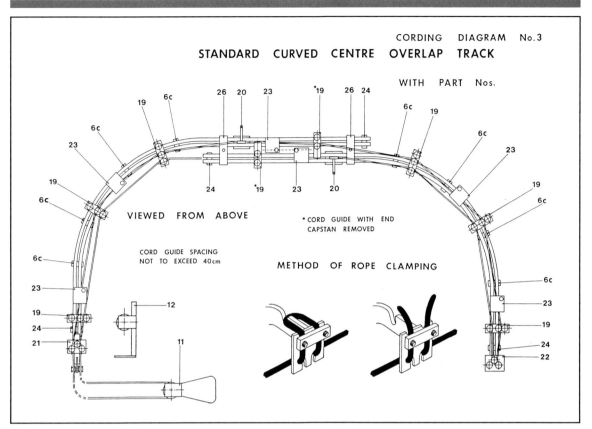

CORDING   DIAGRAM   No.3

STANDARD   CURVED   CENTRE   OVERLAP   TRACK

WITH   PART   Nos.

VIEWED   FROM   ABOVE

*CORD GUIDE WITH END
CAPSTAN REMOVED

CORD   GUIDE   SPACING
NOT   TO   EXCEED   40cm

METHOD   OF   ROPE   CLAMPING

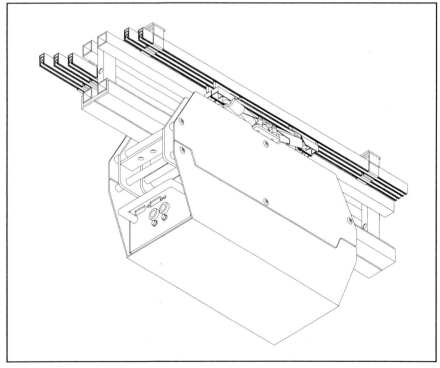

replaced by an electrical device which does the pulling and does away with the necessity of the cords.

This is particularly useful where the track is following a circuitous or twisting path (see illustrations 2.8, 2.9 on page 25 and colour illustration 2).

A 'wipe' is a device whereby one passes a cloth or gauze laterally in front of the audience, usually downstage, with the object being to change the 'picture' of the stage behind the wipe. The wipe emerges from one side of the stage and crosses over to the other where it gathers. There have been instances whereby the wipe which has been used is actually narrower than the proscenium opening, requiring people involved in doing the change to march on behind the wipe cloth, putting things down and picking things up as they move along with it, and as the wipe proceeds a different picture is left, whilst at no point during the course of this effect has the entirety of the stage 'picture' been obscured from the audience.

A wipe can be created by using an ordinary curtain or tab track, some of which have proprietary fittings available to convert them into wiping tracks. The essential characteristic of a wipe is, naturally, that when the leading part of the wipe cloth reaches the end of its travel, the succeeding bobbins rear-fold themselves onto the leading one in the wing until they have all left the area of audience vision. Rear-folding is the common term used for wiping when applied to the mechanical structure provided. It should be possible to reverse the wipe and bring it back across the stage in the opposite direction and use the same technique to once again change the visual appearance of the stage whilst the wipe is in motion. For this effect to work best the wipe cloth must never actually pause while moving.

A diorama is little used these days, but is basically a large cloth with a continuous landscape or other sort of scene painted upon it which traverses laterally across the stage giving the impression that the event is mobile and moving. If used in conjunction with people running or walking, in front of the diorama eg, chariot races, it is particularly effective.

A diorama may be a specific application of a wipe or it may be something rather longer which needs more organisation and arrangement. There have been a few instances of the use of what is called a banjo track where the diorama passes in front of the audience from left to right for instance, and then reverses on itself and comes back again in the other direction revealing the reverse side. The diorama effect was used in *The Travails of Sancho Panza* at the Old Vic, where a gauze two and a half times the width of the stage was employed to travel backwards and forwards, revealing one or more different aspects of itself for different scenes. This was simply effected by using standard curtain track and using spring loaded, counter-opposed wheels to pinch the top of the gauze and pull it this way and that. This system also obviated the use of any actual hauling line, or sash cord, to activate the cloth and maintained a tension on that part of the cloth which was in view of the audience.

Travelators or tappets

These are the rolling staircases, flattened out (such as one now encounters at airports), whereby the impression of movement can be maintained for people running, vehicles travelling, horses galloping, etc. If the people run against the movement of the travelator they give the impression of running whilst not actually moving anywhere. This, allied with a diorama (see above) will give a strong impression or effect of speed and movement.

The use of a large revolve for this effect has also been undertaken whereby someone or some things on the downstage section of the revolve run or travel against the direction of the revolve.

Trucks

The word 'trucks' for this purpose means wheeled items of scenery which are to move in front of the audience. The producer of this effect has to consider the nature of the movement required. It is foolhardy to expect a truck, even with fixed wheels, to consistently travel from and return to the same position. Imperfections in the settings of the wheels, floor surface and the cleanliness of the floor, will all serve to take the truck slowly and increasingly out of position. The more it is proposed to use the truck during the show, the more likely it will have to be guided in some way or another. The simplest guided system of all is to lay sheets of board on the stage floor leaving a narrow gap and provide the truck with a metal bracket which will set into the gap and prevent it slipping from side to side as it travels.

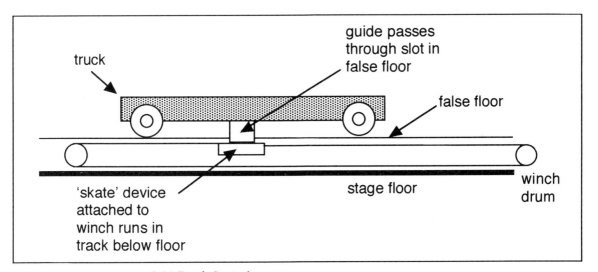

2.10 Truck Control
The system relies on the false floor over the main stage. The mechanism is very much like an inverted tab track with the connection to the truck above being similar to the bobbin of a tab track. The wire needs to be kept taut in order to precisely position the truck and at the same time prevent unwanted movement. Depending on budget, complexity and length of run, different motive power systems can be applied to the winch. The simplest is the manual or hand-wound winch, but the more sophisticated installations have had electrical motors and, more frequently now, hydraulic motors applied, to drive the aforesaid winch.

The simplest way of moving a truck is to get behind it and push. If this is at all practical it will remain the easiest method of doing it. For long running or larger performances a different system is normally employed. This entails laying some kind of additional floor over and above the nominal performance area. Within this there are not only slots for giving guidance to the trucks, but also what is in essence an inverted track whereby a component can be winched back and forth beneath the guidance slot. If one engages an element of the truck to the component beneath the stage (see illustration 2.10 on page 27) then the truck will follow the movement of the lead component of the track. This system, which is normally driven by helical winches, can be driven by manual, electric, or hydraulically powered units. For some performances, smaller items such as individual items of furniture can be treated as trucks when the furniture can be brought to the acting area and struck again by winching to an off-stage, out of sight, position.

It must be consistently borne in mind that successful operation of wheeled effects depends on the clear analysis of the frequency and type of movement, together with available resource and circumstance. Such things as whether the performance area is level or raked may have great bearing on how one intends to operate this kind of effect. It is possible for wheeled units to run down the slope of a rake simply by allowing their own weight to act as the drive. They may then be winched back up the slope or in fact be attached to a counter-weight flying system whereby the counter-weights of the flying system and the flyman pull the truck back up the stage. Experiments should always be carried out if the truck is to move anything other than straight

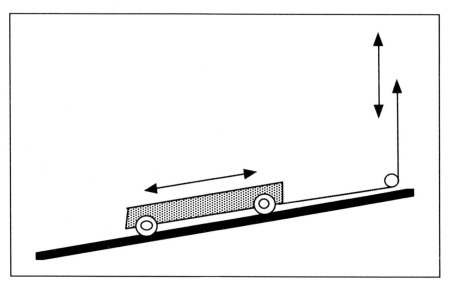

2.11 Flown Truck
A truck with large wheels will run down a raked stage on its own gravity. A winch or counterweight bar (as illustrated) will pull it back upstage.

down the rake. The experiment can be carried out using stage weights and samples of the wheels on which the trucks are to be riding. (See illustration 2.11 on page 28)

Revolves

The earliest revolves were the Greek 'periaktoi', triangular columns which revolved with different scenes on the faces. (See illustration 2.12 below.) The Greeks used these to indicate changes of location and scene and they were placed either side of the Greek or Roman stage. Throughout the centuries the normal scenic presentation was of flat perspective wings which moved laterally to reveal different pictures of scenic artistry. The advent of steel and electricity as readily available products, enabled theatres to install revolving stages. These began around the turn of the century and were initially seen as a means of creating some of the spectacle the Victorians so enjoyed in their theatre. In the 1920s and 1930s when British theatre concentrated more on what became known as 'the well made play' ie, one with three distinct acts in three distinct locations, the revolving stage was used more as a means of facilitating the change between one act and another without having to dismantle and re-erect during the interval. Revolves are fairly easy structures mechanically, given that they simply have to be located, normally by some kind of central pivot, and then driven, normally by some kind of wire rope which runs in a groove around the perimeter of the revolve through to some driving winch that may or may not be electrical.

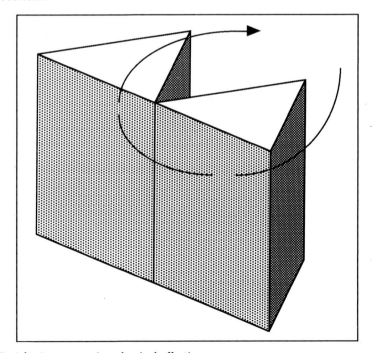

2.12 Periaktoi — a genuine classical effect!
Triangular prisms, each revolving round its own axis, provide three faces with separate visual pictures. They have also been used to present different acoustic surfaces.

However, for small and specific revolves, such as the revolving bed effect in Feydeau's *A Flea in her Ear*, the bedroom in the hotel of ill-repute can quickly be converted into an innocent scene by spinning the bed. The revolve never has to go through three hundred and sixty degrees, but simply pass backwards and forwards through one hundred and eighty degrees. This means it can be activated by pulling, using ropes, from one side or the other, and requires no mechanical drive whatsoever.

Air castors

Air castors are in effect a small hovercraft whereby the weight of the object to be moved sits on a cushion of air which is switched off when the object is in place. Once the object is raised by the air, movement in any direction is easy. However the object can glide some distance immediately the air is removed and this, coupled with the difficulty of lateral precision has tended to restrict the use of this technique to the movement of large objects out of the public's gaze. Some air can also be lost through traps or depressions in the stage causing the object to stick and this also has tended to deter people from using the technique. However there are examples of quite heavy objects being moved in scene changes simply through the application of domestic or small industrial blowers. Fan noise is a problem and thus the movement is best carried out during intervals when heavy house tabs or even safety curtains can mask the noise.

Other effects
Vamps

Vamps are means of effecting sudden appearances or disappearances such as those involving demon kings or magicians (frequently accompanied by puffs of smoke). Instead of taking the vertical path through the stage (see **traps** above) the actor moves horizontally through an aperture in the scenery wall. A lightweight door is held in position with a spring which closes instantly when the person has passed through. Alternatively, strips of elasticated material can be used instead of springs, but cannot be recommended for well lit situations as they may continue to vibrate after the event, giving the game away. Timing is also important and frequently the audience's concentration is manipulated so that it focusses not only physically on the wrong component in the effect, but also at the wrong time so that the actual operation of the effect can take place without suspicion.

Rain

Actual rain is rarely used on the stage for obvious safety reasons. However, there are effects which have been used to simulate the wetness after a rainstorm.

One of the most successful has involved the construction of a trough above a door or window (or whatever) through which the rain is to be seen, which can then be filled with one or two layers of towelling. A hose pipe with holes punctured at intervals can then be laid along the top of the towelling and if water is released into this it soaks through the towelling, down through holes drilled in the base of the trough and gives a realistic drip effect, which may also be heard 'splattering' as it hits whatever catchment receptacle is placed below. NB: with all mechanical effects (rain boxes, rain troughs or thunder runs) one must bear in mind that once the effect has been set in motion, it is not easily halted; it must run its course. This is particularly true of the rain trough just mentioned. (The use of projected rain and alternative mechanical methods are described on pages 123–4.)

Thunder run

Technically this is a sound effect. However, it was a common enough piece of stage equipment for many years. Wooden troughs were set on a slope so that cannon balls could rumble down them, recreating the noise of thunder. Variation was controlled by the frequency of ball despatch. (See illustration 2.13)

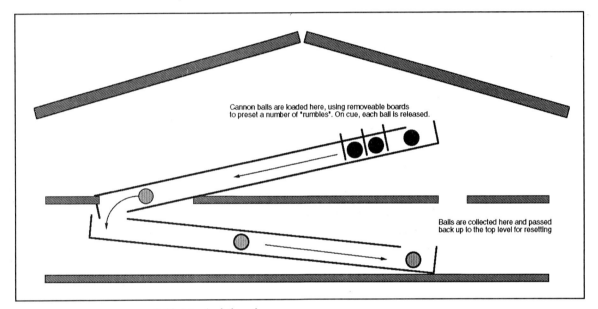

Cannon balls are loaded here, using removeable boards to preset a number of "rumbles". On cue, each ball is released.

Balls are collected here and passed back up to the top level for resetting

2.13 A typical thunder-run.

Things that drop or break

There are a myriad of little things that are often required to happen onstage to make even the outwardly simplest play work. For example, in Noel Coward's *Hay Fever*, a 'straight' comedy, a barometer has to fall off the wall on cue. There is no shortage of this sort of gag in the catalogue of English plays. Space will not allow the examination in detail of every type of trick but some of the more popular ones will prove useful as guidelines.

One such example is breaking furniture eg, where the chair has to break under the weight of the 'fat' person. A good prop maker will want to know if the gag is the reaction of the character or the damage to the chair. In the latter case, it is essential for the chair to break as spectacularly as possible ie, all the legs and bits splayed out in all directions, or just the seat stove through. First, select the chair. If the legs are to splay, separate all the joints if it is made of wood. Remove traces of glue. Press fit it all together again. Lean on it. Watch how it breaks. Use of judgement is required now to decide how much of it is to break ie, does it want to fall completely to pieces, or just one leg give way. Solidly fix bits that want to stay put and press fit, or lightly adhere, the joints to break. More than one experiment will be needed.

The above illustration will not give a satisfying noise of splitting wood. If this is a prerequisite, then one or two of the chair's normal components will have to be replaced with something more brittle – balsa or obeche, which may need to be partially sawn through. Plywood makes a very satisfactory rending noise and, shaped per the real chair part, may well fit the bill.

Much of the above logic needs to be pursued for breaking bannisters etc. It cannot be overstated that any 'breakaway' of this nature must be considered as a 'one-off'. Contingent factors such as frequency, length of run, performer dexterity, and allowable mess factor, need to be taken into account in each instance.

Things that fall tend to be simpler. Things that fall off the set are usually 'nudged' or have their suspension quickly taken away eg, picture cord can rest on a dowel set in the scenery. When the dowel is drawn back the picture falls.

Some objects are required to fall 'from a great height', plummeting into view. (See illustration 2.14)

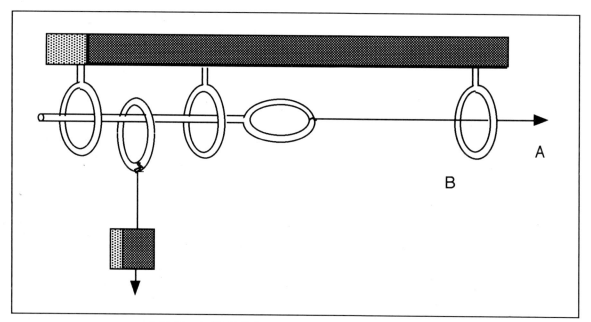

2.14 Simple Trick Release
The line 'A' when pulled moves as far back as 'B' which releases the suspended object. The line is prevented from falling into view by being held at 'B'. A similar mechanism can release the base of boxes suspended over the stage and containing small items such as balls and fruit (in panto!).

When planning a release mechanism, it is worth remembering that a chain is only as strong as its weakest link. Thread, paper etc, will break if given a sharp tug. This is very useful, provided the thread can support the weight of what is to fall until it is 'tugged'.

Falling snow, balloons, rubble and more random items are most easily dealt with by a variant of the traditional snow bag. (See illustration 2.15)

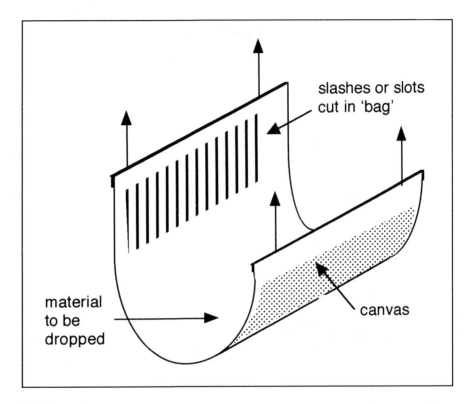

2.15 Snow Bag
Traditional release mechanisms for random objects to fall from above. The 'snow', or whatever, lies in the solid side of the bag until the set of lines attached to the other side are lowered, rolling the objects towards and through the slots. Sensitively operated the snow bag can provide variations of fall over a period of time.

Really frantic farce, with lots of down slamming may benefit from the use of 'Marie Tempests'. These devices ensure that the door stays precisely where the actors leave it – open, ajar, shut, etc. (see illustration 2.16 on page 34). What is wanted is a simple door check with a friction washer which will need regular adjustment. The advantages to the performers are considerable: the door stays in the position the actor leaves it in and never moves on its own thereby upstaging the hard working performers.

Animatronics   Much sophisticated work is being done in the field on animatronics. These are the moving models one sees at waxworks and theme parks. Basically,

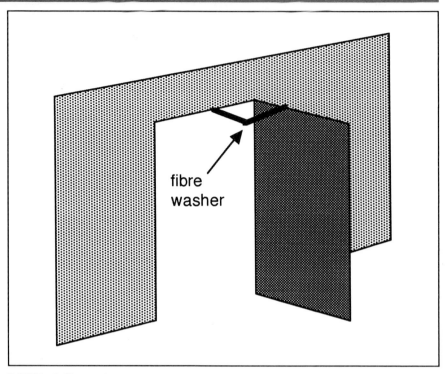

2.16 Marie Tempest
A lightweight door or window check with a fibre washer attached as shown, stops the door wherever it is put. The door will not swing randomly and distract the audience, very useful in farce.

what are being developed are pneumatic muscles. These are being allied to the rubber latex puppets popularised on television. This is a form of work which, despite its apparent success, is probably still in its infancy. Small animations can be constructed and powered from the more sophisticated parts of children's toys which frequently rely on modular components and electrical or pneumatic power supplies. The use of such models, as large performers on stage, can produce satisfactory results. However, the live stage presentation cannot use the computer generated or enhanced movement of the cinematic variety.

ENDPIECE

My personal awareness of effects came rather slowly. Since childhood my abiding memory of my first pantomine was of Aladdin sparkling in the cave. I now know that she was covered in sequins and being followed by an arc lamp. I wouldn't think of it as special now, just as part of our technical armoury.

As a young professional, I was deeply struck by the sight of several small flats flying together. They were all attached to the drum and shaft (see earlier illustration on page 23) at the Theatre Royal Bristol. They moved slowly against a dark background and had an ethereal, almost magical quality as they landed and then flew out from different levels in complete synchronisation.

At the Old Vic, for *Much Ado About Nothing*, Zefferelli wanted to change the wing flats instantly as of the eighteenth century, but it didn't quite work. Without the substage mechanism linking the flats, we had to rely on eight stage crew and four flymen for each change and, despite their excellence, the precision was impossible to achieve on a regular basis.

A lot probably depends upon subjective response. For Brecht's *Baal* starring Peter O'Toole at the Phoenix Theatre London, designed by Jocelyn Herbert, lighting by Richard Pilbrow and projections by Robert Ornbo, a vast 48ft high wrap round cyc was installed. Flown pieces were run directly to the counter-weight system and the proscenium was the only border. When the cyc was washed with subtle projected backgrounds the effect was of vast space, as though the stage were limitless and the proscenium opening truly became a window on another world.

Effects are also a product of necessity. In a very successful production of *Trojan Women* at the Theatre Royal, Stratford East, London, Cassandra was plotted to carry an extinguished torch. A cavity was made to contain a smoke pellet or similar device. Then in rehearsal the lady started to swing the torch about through 360°. A new idea was necessary. The stage management sought the advice of a local chemist who devised a compound which, when lit, not only smoked, but also became glutinous and stuck itself to whatever surface it was on. Cassandra could now do what she liked with her torch, which trailed smoke wherever she swung it. As the lighting designer, I had plenty on my plate without chasing chemists for magic formulae. I wish I had done so.

In the end, however, I think that the technician has to have a facility for taking a calculated risk. With regard to *Back to Methuselah* (see illustrations 2.17, 2.18, 2.19 on page 37) at the Old Vic, London, the manufacturers, ICI, told us that they doubted the wisdom of suspending 20ft sheets of perspex. In the end, we decided that all the evidence we could gather led us to think that it would be possible and so despite the views of the manufacturer, we went ahead and were successful. I think that this, more than anything else, has to be the benchmark by which successful technicians can be measured, that is to say they have to receive the evidence, draw their conclusions, and make their bets.

2.17 2.18 2.19

An example of a successful effect was used in the opening sequence to the National Theatre production of *Back to Methuselah* (1969) directed by Clifford Williams, designed by Ralph Koltai, with lighting by Robert Ornbo, production managed by Joe Aveline. The audience initially saw a gauze with central emblem painted onto it. The central emblem was then subjected to a projected device from front of house (ie, audience side) and then a light change allowed the gauze to become translucent and the audience saw through it a series of suspended spheres. As the gauze was tumbled out, a large ball on a pole (not unlike an oversized toffee apple) revolved as though it were the Earth spinning through space amongst the suspended spheres. Hanging in the centre of the stage was a black disc with a shiny perspex rim. The revolving sphere (Earth) stopped downstage and then started to move upstage towards the centre of the revolve. As it moved, the black sphere together with attendant lighting was flown out to reveal a delicate transparent and green crescent shape into which the moving sphere eventually settled. At this point it was precisely over the centre of the revolve and able to revolve again as it now resembled the tree of good and evil in the Garden of Eden.

This sequence, which represented the beginning of time consistently received a round of applause from the audience before the first words of the play between Adam and Eve were ever spoken. It caught the imagination, especially so because this was, after all, the year in which man first set foot on the moon.

This sequence required extremely precise cueing of lighting, revolve, the moving earth and the flies. It should be noted that the only person able to see all these activities would be the stage manager giving cues. The co-ordinating role was pivotol to the success of the enterprise. The whole sequence took quite a long time and was accompanied by appropriate sounds. It was made possible because it had been conceived in total at an early stage. It was not the result of random happenstance and every single facet of the complex procedure had been present at the very earliest discussions of how the play was to begin. We have noted it here as perhaps a caution to those wishing to undertake complex effects that they must have envisaged the entire sequence before undertaking to produce the hardware and the software that actually makes them take place.

This sequence, as described, had to be established in such a way that it could fit into the normal repertoire changeover routine of the National Theatre at the Old Vic. The theatre had been adapted with a forestage established downstage of the iron curtain. The gauze was suspended in this area, where there was no flying height, and therefore it had to be tumbled (see page 17) rather than flown out and this was accomplished with the aid of an electric winch. The stage floor was raked to 1:16 which provided a geometric problem with the location of the revolving Earth over the centre pin of the revolve where an adequate tolerance had to be allowed between it and the surrounding flying piece. The movement of the Earth on its pole was accomplished by a winch located underneath the stage pulling a wire which lay across the floor of the revolve. No tracking or guidance system was used. Plastic skids (similar to those found on a sledge) were attached to the base of the pole which supported the Earth. These skids enabled the structure to slide across the fabric floor surface. The advantage of this was that it was less likely to deviate from its course than wheels. But more importantly there was absolutely no likelihood of the skids, when the motion was stopped, backsliding by even a fraction. It also meant that as the revolve moved the friction of the skids was adequate to maintain the object in place without the need for brakes.

2.18 above right.

The opening sequence of *Back to Methuselah*
The 'Earth' seen on a pole in illustration 2.18 is
revolving through space in illustration 2.17 and
revolves again within the Tree of Good and Evil
in illustration 2.19 by which time it has moved
from the rim to the centre of the revolve.

2.19

3 Sound Effects

JOHN LEONARD

SOUND DESIGN The term 'Sound Designer' has only come in to common usage in the past twenty years or so. That does not mean to say that there were no sound designers before that time, but simply that they were called something else. Sound technician, sound engineer or simply sound man, although the latter carries slightly pejorative connotations in some countries. Whatever the title, and I use it here for convenience only, the principles involved in bringing to fruition the realisation of a soundtrack for a show has been the same for many years; only the equipment and techniques have changed.

WHY DO WE NEED SOUND EFFECTS?

We have already seen that in Shakespeare's time sound effects were not always necessary (see page 6). Much information can be given to the audience by way of textual references or by the way that the actors behave on the stage. If an actor declares 'I came here by car, the Rolls actually!', then there is little need for the audience to have heard the effect of a Rolls Royce arriving off-stage. If another character arrives in a scene visibly wet, carrying an umbrella and states 'What terrible weather we are having at the moment', there is not actually a requirement for the sound of rain to be heard.

What are the reasons for using sound effects? We can break them down into a number of categories, but here are the most usual ones.

1) *Information*:   the audience needs to be told something about period, location, time of day and time of year, and external events that may be relevant, or the state of the weather. Modern authors have a tendency to write stage directions that read something like this: 'The play opens in a deserted warehouse near a freight yard in Seattle in 1933. It is late evening on a bitterly cold winter's night'. These details may be very important to an audience's understanding of a play and it will be up to the scenic designer, the sound designer and the lighting designer to give the audience the clues that it needs.

2) *Textual reference*:   sounds which are referred to or reacted to by characters in a production. These can range from the mundane, such as toilet flushes, to the ethereal, such as the 'twang' in *The Cherry Orchard*, to the monumental such as the avalanche at the end of *When We Dead Awaken*.

3) *Mood creation*:   any sound that creates an atmosphere that may not be suggested in the text, but complements the underlying mood of the piece; wind whistling through a crack, in a horror story for example, or the sound of the factory sirens in a gritty northern drama.

4) *Emotional stimulus*:   sounds that play on knee-jerk emotional reactions and sometimes physical reactions from an audience – loud bangs, heartbeats, piercing metallic scrapings, squeal of car brakes, high-level low-frequency rumbles, comic effects, although these must be handled with care, (not all audiences share the same sense of humour).

5) *Cues to reinforce on-stage action*:   telephones, doorbells, door knocks, domestic fires etc.

Many plays will require effects from a cross-section of the above categories:

as an example, I would like to refer to a play by Nicholas Wright called, *The Desert Air*.

The play was produced at The Royal Shakespeare Company's studio theatre in Stratford-Upon-Avon, directed by Bill Alexander and was set in Africa during the Second World War. The play opens on the parade ground of a British army camp somewhere in the North African desert and continues in and around the camp, during the period of one week. There are scenes that take place indoors, outdoors, in a house of ill-repute, in a night club, in a car and in the desert itself and the play has a stage direction towards the end of the first page which simply reads, 'The doors of the theatre open and an invisible Sherman tank drives onto the stage'. A little later in the text, Field Marshall Montgomery taps on the hull of the invisible tank, and holds a conversation with the (equally invisible) driver. This rather odd sequence was inspired by the fact that the Allies sought the help of an illusionist, Victor Maskelyne, to help them disguise their tanks during the fighting in North Africa.

The play opened with a bare stage with the sound of soldiers carrying out parade ground drill in the background, a distant gramophone playing songs of the period and an atmosphere track of insects. A bright lighting state reveals the stage. The audience is thus informed that the following scene is set in or near a military establishment, probably outdoors in a hot climate during daylight hours in the 1940s. Gradually, soldiers drift onto the stage and the actor portraying Montgomery arrives to start the proceedings. His opening speech gives more precise information about the location and time in which the play is set.

'The doors of the theatre open, and an invisible tank comes onto the stage'. This effect was achieved by the simple method of having the 'tank' start its engine off-stage; a cloud of exhaust fumes from a smoke machine is blowing onto the stage as the double doors leading directly onto the stage open and the sound effect is slowly panned from the external speaker onto speakers in the centre of the theatre. The effect is played at a high level and contains sufficient low-frequency information to affect the audience physically ie, they feel the sound as well as hearing it. The tank stops, the smoke gradually clears and there is complete silence. Montgomery leans forward, raises his swagger stick and raps the air in front of him. We hear the sound of the stick hitting the tank in sync with the actor's movements. The cast applaud and Montgomery congratulates the inventor, who is driving the tank. We hear 'Thank you very much, sir' in a muffled voice from thin air, and the tank is started up and driven back out of the theatre with the help of a little more smoke. Gradually during the course of the scene, the insects start up again and play until the next scene, which is an interior.

In the opening of the script, therefore, we have an example of sound effects giving the audience information about the location and period of the action, creating the invisible tank referred to in the script, providing a sound effect to correspond with an action, and intentionally, making the audience laugh, which the muffled voice-over invariably succeeded in doing. During the rest of the play, many other sound effects were used in conjunction with specially composed music played by a small band, lighting changes and the minimum of props and furniture, to suggest all other locations in the play.

USE OF MUSIC

The use of music can contribute a great deal to a production. Music may be either specially composed, chosen from the commercially available recordings or, in some cases, chosen from the specialist music libraries that commission works from composers to cover many different moods and situations for use in film, television and radio. Many talented composers write and record music for these specialist libraries and it is sometimes possible to find music that reflects exactly the mood that you may be trying to create. These companies will sometimes license theatres to use their recordings, although you may expect to have to pay quite high fees for this permission. Names of the major libraries are given in the appendix.

It is essential for the sound designer to have at least a passing knowledge of many different types of music, from Renaissance dance music through ethnic folk music, ancient and modern classical, all forms of jazz, blues swing, rock and roll, middle of the road, strict tempo dance, to current styles of mainstream and independent label pop music. A quick glance through my own collection reveals such delights as Spanish baroque organ music, collected sea shanties and nautical songs, The Grimethorpe Colliery Band, a French album of circus music, classical works from Albinoni to Xenakis and Zemlinsky, The Beatles, The Monkees, Howlin' Wolf, John Lee Hooker, Eric Clapton, Julian Bream, Nigel Kennedy, Stephan Grapelli, Stephen Sondheim, The Mormon Tabernacle choir and literally hundreds more artists and composers famous and obscure. Most of these records have been purchased either for use in shows, or because they might one day be useful in a show.

Choosing music for use in a play can be an immensely rewarding experience but it requires patience and knowledge and a degree of research. The director will have his or her own ideas about what is required and the process of refining and elimination can be a lengthy one. A production of a play with a few critical music cues can require as much time to research and prepare as one that has many more, but less important cues, and the sound designer must be prepared to spend large amounts of time in record shops and libraries gathering material for presentation to the director.

Taste in music is completely subjective and it can be daunting to have your own choices condemned by a director who does not share your taste; however, beware of letting either your own or your director's taste lead you into using music that is inappropriate simply because it is a favourite piece. Gentle persuasion is often the only course to take in such circumstances; finding something better is ideal.

A director may decide to employ a composer to write music especially for the production. This is an ideal situation, although there is an increasing tendency to use music in theatre as aural wallpaper; I suspect that this has come about through exposure to film and television scores, where bad plots are upholstered by music scores that are intended solely to manipulate the emotions of an audience when the dramatic action fails to do so. The use of electronic synthesisers and samplers has meant large-scale sounding musical scores can be realised without the cost of employing live musicians: it can also lead to gratuitous use of music, simply because it is easy and cheap to achieve and can, in my opinion, be counter-productive.

The involvement of live musicians in a theatrical production as part of the production team can be a tremendous asset. If it is seen that a particular piece is not working, a competent team of musicians can make changes very rapidly and try the music a different way. Similarly, if music cues need to be shortened or lengthened to fit on-stage action, a musical director and a live band can adapt quickly to these requirements. It is essential for the sound designer and/or operator to be considered a part of the musical team on shows that have specially composed scores; the sound team needs to be aware of what effect the composer intends the music to have and the composer, musical director and musicians must feel that the sound team is on their side, working to represent them in the best possible way, particularly when the musicians are working in an off-stage studio with no direct contact with the performance. Good manners should ensure that they are kept informed about why they are being asked to alter their performances, or why delays are occurring. There is nothing worse than a musician being asked to sit in a studio for several hours without knowing what is happening on-stage. Audio and video relay of stage action should always be provided in these situations so that those who wish to see and hear what is happening can do so. You will invariably get a better performance from an interested musician than you will from one who is bored stiff.

If restrictions on finances or space seem to dictate that specially composed music has to be recorded, it should be noted that the permission should be sought, in the United Kingdom at least, of the Musician's Union (MU), who impose a number of restrictions on the use of recorded music for theatre. I have always found that early contact with the MU and a reasoned argument will achieve the desired result. Once again, you will obtain maximum co-operation from your musicians if you make them fully aware of how the music that they are going to record for you is to be used.

Often directors will want to attend recording sessions to make sure that the arrangements are correct for the productions. If a large amount of music is to be recorded, then multi-track tape recorders should be used, rather than recording direct to stereo. It is always less expensive to re-mix a music track to obtain a better balance than it is to have to re-record the entire session. On a number of occasions, I have brought a multi-track machine into the theatre and balanced the music during technical rehearsals, recording the resultant mix to stereo at the same time. A sound designer should therefore have a basic knowledge of music theory as he or she may have to supervise or carry out these recording sessions or to edit or re-arrange commercial recorded music. The ability to follow a music score is required when balancing or adding effects in a musical production and an understanding of basic musical terms is useful when discussing the operation of a show with a composer or musician.

NB There is an increasing tendency for composers to produce their own music and sound effects tracks for productions and for sound designers to become composers. Providing that the individual concerned is sufficiently talented in each of these two areas then such an integration can work extremely well. However all concerned need to be sure that the requirements of one discipline do not impinge on the requirements of the other. If more changes need to be made to a soundtrack, then it can be much more helpful if one person can concentrate on the sound effects whilst the other concentrates on the music.

Copyright

The use of copyright music in a theatre production also involves obtaining the necessary permission and often paying a licensing fee to the copyright holder. Fortunately, in the United Kingdom these procedures are handled by three organisations; the Performing Rights Society (PRS) who handle permission to perform the copyright work; the Mechanical Copyright Protection Society (MCPS), who license the copying of recorded music; and Phonographic Performances Ltd (PPL) who licence the use of recorded music in public. MCPS and PPL will issue blanket licences to the theatre or organisation concerned, but PRS require that a return form is filled in with precise details of music used, duration and the number of performances. The addresses of these organisations are listed in the appendix. Many theatre companies use copyright music without consulting any of these organisations and without paying copyright fees and are thus in breach of copyright laws: registering the music you use is not a long process and is the only way that composers can be sure of receiving payment for use of their work. A sample PRS return form is illustrated on page 44.

Stereo recordings

The use of stereo recordings of effects and music can enhance a soundtrack in a number of ways, even though the majority of the audience will not be in the ideal listening position. Problems may occur in the use of stereo music with a particularly wide sound stage for those sitting in extreme side seats, but such recordings are rare. Stereo recordings are useful for 'moving' sound effects like traffic, but can also add realism to many other atmospheric effects such as wind, rain, birdsong or sea.

Some 'moving' sound effects are best left in mono, and moved from speaker to speaker using desk output faders or joystick controllers. The complex helicopter sequence in the musical *Miss Saigon* is controlled by a set of automated moving faders: the operator moves the faders during rehearsals at the required rate for each part of the sequence, and the fader moves are recorded by a microprocessor controlled memory system. Each set of moves is recorded as a cue, assigned a number and stored in a non-

T 028224

PROGRAMME AND DECLARATION OF MUSIC (PLAYS)

The Performing Right Society Limited

An Association of Composers, Authors and Publishers of Music

29/33 BERNERS STREET, LONDON W1P 4AA   TELEPHONE 071-580 5544

Nature of production (play or compilation show) _____ entitled _____

Theatre premises: Name _____

Address _____

No. of performances (incl. previews) _____ in run from _____ 19 ___ to _____ 19 ___ (if a tour please attach itinerary)

Means of performance: Live (e.g. band, pianist, vocalist)

Recorded (e.g. tape, record player)

Status of production: amateur or professional

See notes overleaf

For PRS use

1. Programme number

2. Tariff

3. Geographical code

4. Account number

5. Royalty   £

For PRS use (line no)	OVERTURE, ENTR'ACTE or EXIT music TITLE OF MUSICAL WORK (block capitals)	Times played each performance	Duration	COMPOSER(S) (surname(s) first)	PUBLISHER	ARRANGER	For PRS use
1							
2							
3							
4							
5							
6							
7							
8							
9							
	INCIDENTAL or CURTAIN music (heard by theatre audience but not performed by or intended to be audible to characters).						
10							
11							
12							
13							
14							
15							
16							
17							
18							

IMPORTANT — The declarations on the back of this form must be completed.

PRS

GIVING MUSIC ITS DUE

3.1 PRS form.

volatile memory until it is recalled for playback. Servomotors then reproduce the operator's fader movements in response to each cue. This system has the advantage over other automatic fader systems with Voltage Controlled Amplifiers that the operator has an instant visual check on the progress of a fade and access to the faders, should the need arise.

Experiments with surround-sound systems, such as Ambisonics™, have proved to be successful under controlled circumstances, but few theatre companies have investigated their use with any degree of enthusiasm. The lead may come from cinemas and theme parks which are using enhanced stereo systems, such as Dolby Surround™ and Roland 3D™
, to add realism to their presentations.

Multi-tracked effects   Multi-channel replay devices, such as multi-track tape recorders, both analogue and digital, and multiple-output samplers, can also be useful in creating realistic effects sequences. A fierce storm at sea, for example, can have a large number of component parts: wind, thunder, rain, crashing waves and creaking timbers. Rather than produce a fixed mix of all the effects on one tape, it is often better to isolate each element on one track or output of the replay device, and mix the effects in situ. An example of a multiple output plot is shown in illustration 3.2 on pages 46–7. The designer can then vary the content and ferocity of the storm as the action of the play demands. This can save constant re-mixing of composite tracks when the balance needs to be changed.

PREPARATIONS FOR THE SHOW   There is a sequence of events that needs to take place prior to any preparation of a music and effects track for a production.

The first requirement is to read the script: this may seem like an obvious statement, but it is necessary to have a working knowledge of the style of the play before you start taking note of any effects detailed or implied in the text. Next, a discussion with the director should reveal the style in which this is to be presented. This a very important meeting, where much can be revealed about how much the sound designer is going to have to contribute to a production. I have attended preliminary meetings with directors where it has been revealed to me that a production of *Julius Caesar* is to take place in the twenty-first century, or that a production of *The Revenger's Tragedy* is to be updated to 1930s New York. It is also at this meeting that the director's feelings about music will be expressed and whether a composer is going to be a part of the creative team. Following this meeting, the list of effects gathered from the reading of the script may need to be radically altered, but it does mean that a start can be made in gathering possible sounds. The result of the first meeting with the director will also trigger other meetings – with the designer and the lighting designer to discuss practical considerations such as siting of loudspeakers or microphones, with the composer to discuss how information is to be passed on and updated, and whether there

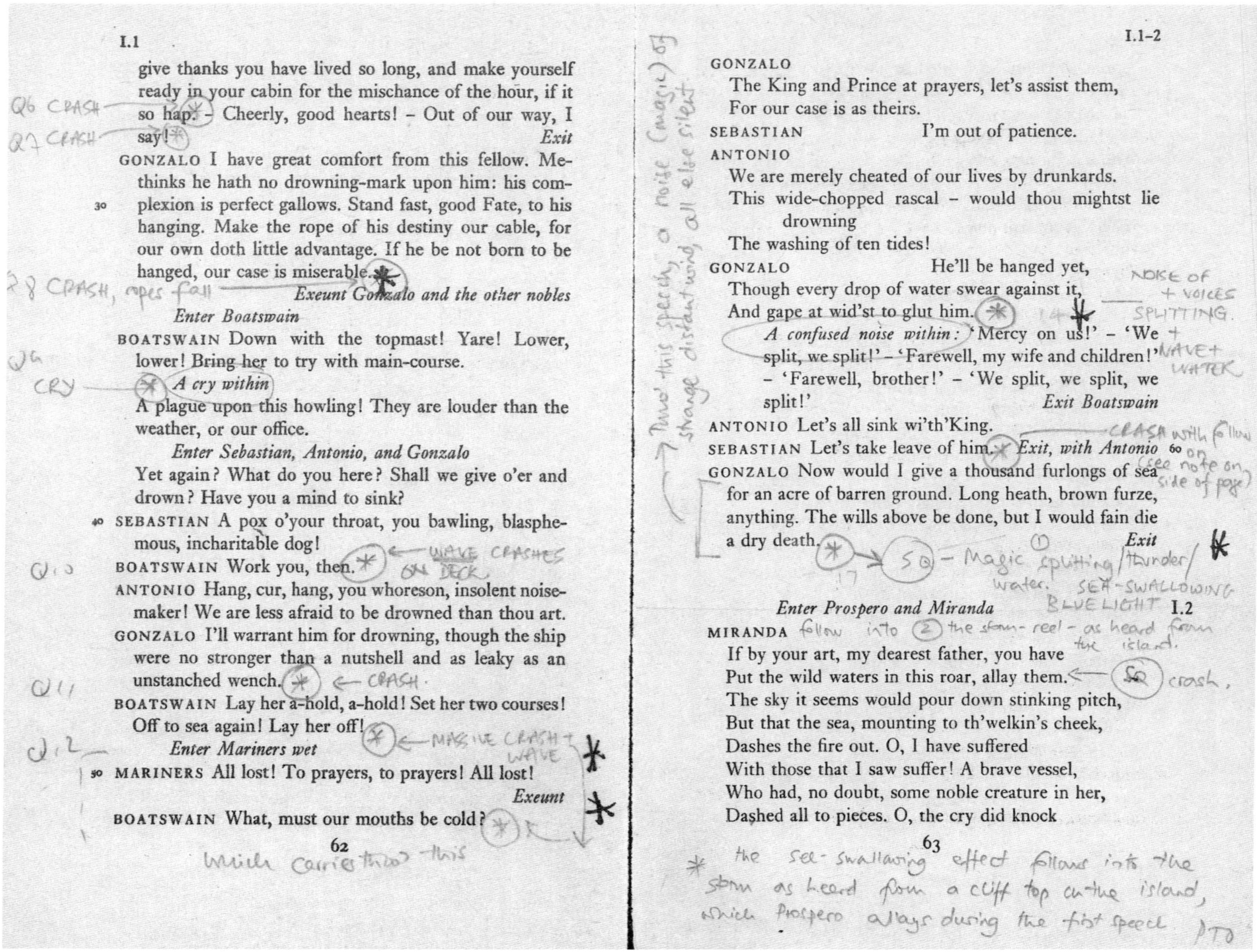

I.1

give thanks you have lived so long, and make yourself
ready in your cabin for the mischance of the hour, if it
so hap. – Cheerly, good hearts! – Out of our way, I
say!   *Exit*

GONZALO I have great comfort from this fellow. Me-
thinks he hath no drowning-mark upon him: his com-
plexion is perfect gallows. Stand fast, good Fate, to his
hanging. Make the rope of his destiny our cable, for
our own doth little advantage. If he be not born to be
hanged, our case is miserable.   *Exeunt Gonzalo and the other nobles*

Enter Boatswain
BOATSWAIN Down with the topmast! Yare! Lower,
lower! Bring her to try with main-course.   *A cry within*
A plague upon this howling! They are louder than the
weather, or our office.
Enter Sebastian, Antonio, and Gonzalo
Yet again? What do you here? Shall we give o'er and
drown? Have you a mind to sink?
SEBASTIAN A pox o'your throat, you bawling, blasphe-
mous, incharitable dog!
BOATSWAIN Work you, then.
ANTONIO Hang, cur, hang, you whoreson, insolent noise-
maker! We are less afraid to be drowned than thou art.
GONZALO I'll warrant him for drowning, though the ship
were no stronger than a nutshell and as leaky as an
unstanched wench.
BOATSWAIN Lay her a-hold, a-hold! Set her two courses!
Off to sea again! Lay her off!
Enter Mariners wet
MARINERS All lost! To prayers, to prayers! All lost!   *Exeunt*
BOATSWAIN What, must our mouths be cold?

(line numbers 30, 40, 50; page 62)

(Handwritten cue annotations in margin: Q6 CRASH; Q7 CRASH; Q8 CRASH, ropes fall; Q9 CRY; Q10 — ON DECK / WAVE CRASHES; Q11 ← CRASH; Q12 ← MASSIVE CRASH + WAVE; WAVE CRASH THRO' THIS)

I.1-2

GONZALO
The King and Prince at prayers, let's assist them,
For our case is as theirs.
SEBASTIAN   I'm out of patience.
ANTONIO
We are merely cheated of our lives by drunkards.
This wide-chopped rascal – would thou mightst lie
    drowning
The washing of ten tides!
GONZALO   He'll be hanged yet,
Though every drop of water swear against it,
And gape at wid'st to glut him.
A confused noise within: 'Mercy on us!' – 'We –
split, we split!' – 'Farewell, my wife and children!'
– 'Farewell, brother!' – 'We split, we split, we
split!'
ANTONIO Let's all sink wi'th'King.   *Exit*
SEBASTIAN Let's take leave of him.   *Exit, with Antonio*
GONZALO Now would I give a thousand furlongs of sea
for an acre of barren ground. Long heath, brown furze,
anything. The wills above be done, but I would fain die
a dry death.   *Exit*

Exit Boatswain

Enter Prospero and Miranda   1.2
MIRANDA
If by your art, my dearest father, you have
Put the wild waters in this roar, allay them.
The sky it seems would pour down stinking pitch,
But that the sea, mounting to th'welkin's cheek,
Dashes the fire out. O, I have suffered
With those that I saw suffer! A brave vessel,
Who had, no doubt, some noble creature in her,
Dashed all to pieces. O, the cry did knock

(page 63)

(Handwritten annotations: NOISE OF + VOICES / SPLITTING; WAVE + WATER; Magic splitting / thunder / water; SEA-SWALLOWING / BLUE LIGHT; CRASH with (flim); SFX crash; "the sea-swallowing effect fades into the storm as heard from a cliff top on the island, which Prospero plays during the first speech.")

3.2 Effects plot and play text from *The Tempest* showing where cues go.

Cue #	Page	Tape 1	Tape 2	Tape 3	Tape 4
1	61	Magic Noise			Storm Background
2	61		Thunder #1		
3	61			Thunder #2	
4	61	Wind blast			
5	61		Wave crash		
6	62			Thunder #3	
7	62	Thunder #4			
8	62		Ropes crash		
9	62			Bosun cry!	
10	62	Wave crash 2			
11	62		Thunder #5		
12	62	Wave crash 3		Big crash	
13	63		Thunder #6	Voices	
14	63	Split #1	Split #2		
15	63	Rocks crash	Wave #4		
16	63			Magic noise	
17	63	Distant storm	Rumble		
18	63			Waves	

is a need for any practicals ie, televisions, radios, hi-fi systems, or telephones that have to work on stage.

Next, some practical decisions for the sound designer. Are there any effects that need to be live? Door sounds, crashing glass and gun shots are often best produced live in the wings rather than being reproduced artificially. Who will be operating the show? Does the director expect sound in rehearsals? Are there any special equipment considerations that need to be taken into account and how should they be budgeted for? Obvious though it may seem, this sequence of events is often ignored or short-circuited, usually because of a lack of time, and the result is often the creation of a much greater workload for the sound designer in the last few weeks.

During the course of rehearsals, the flow of information needs to be maintained: regular meetings should be scheduled to allow the director to hear and approve work in progress and production meetings, where all the production team can discuss problems arising, should be organised on a weekly basis.

In an ideal world, by the end of a rehearsal period, the soundtrack is complete, the music is written and, if necessary, recorded, and the designer has attended sufficient rehearsals to be confident of placement and length of cues. In some cases, the soundtrack may have been developed in rehearsal, so the actors are used to the sounds and music that are being used in the production. The operator too will have a much more developed sense of how the show fits together and technical rehearsals, the process whereby all technical aspects of the show are rehearsed, should become much less fraught. Conversely, I have worked with directors who reserve the right to keep their options open until as late as possible, making alterations to the sound and music tracks right up to opening night. Whilst this can be an immensely stimulating way of working for the director and designer, it can be confusing and distracting for the cast who have to cope with a soundtrack that is never the same two nights running. Once again, good manners dictate that actors should be informed if any changes are to be made in a soundtrack that may affect their performance.

RECORDING AND PLAYBACK

Until recently, all theatre work has been carried out using analogue magnetic tape recorders. Cues were arranged in order on a master reel, to be played back in sequence, or individually onto NAB standard endless loop cartridges to be played back as required. Often, a combination of these two methods would give the desired flexibility with reel-to-reel equipment handling long music or atmosphere tracks, and cartridges being used for spot effects or looped atmosphere tracks. Today's sound designer has a bewildering choice of equipment to choose from. In terms of recording and playback, one can choose from reel-to-reel analogue tape recorders, NAB analogue cartridge machines, two different types of digital cartridge machine, digital audio tape in one of the many configurations of either rotary or stationary head systems, recordable compact disc and solid state/hard disk storage devices, both stand alone and integrated into personal computer systems.

The format chosen can have a big influence on the way that the soundtrack is assembled, and we should therefore examine each system in some detail. See **Samplers**, page 75 for further discussion.

Reel-to-reel

Reel-to-reel has been, for many years, the only viable choice, along with NAB cartridge machines, for theatre use. Cues are recorded to tape, edited and assembled into a show tape, using lengths of leader tape to separate each cue. (Illustration 3.3)

TAPE   CLEAR   Cue 1 - Opening Music   LEADER

3.3 A method of organising effects for replay during a production. The clear tape is used on Revox and Studer tape machines, where it activates a photo-electric cell which stops the tape just before the sound effect. Other tape machines use reflective tape, or small pieces of metallised tape to control this function.

The leader tape serves to separate and identify the different effects. Identification can be written on the leader with a fine-tipped marking pen.

Some tape machines have sensors that, with the addition of either a small piece of transparent leader tape or a small piece of adhesive metallic foil, will automatically stop the tape ready for the next cue to be played. For some machines, it is possible to purchase such a sensor as an add-on piece of equipment.

The problem with most reel-to-reel machines is that they are noisy in operation: the 'clunk' of a solenoid preceding a quiet background effect can destroy a carefully built-up atmosphere instantly. Some machines can be modified for a relatively quiet start, and some theatres locate their machines remote from the operator in soundproof cabinets.

For many years the preferred tape speed in theatres has been 7.5i.p.s.– 19cm/s following a somewhat misguided principle that this would give greater economy. The gains in quality from recording and playing back at 15i.p.s–38cm/s. far outweigh any slight savings that can be made in tape costs. The higher speed is the standard for broadcast and recording and there is no reason that theatre should be any different.

NAB cartridge (or 'cart') machines

Originally produced for use in the broadcast industry, the NAB cartridge has found a place in theatre because of its noise-free instant start, small size, and the ability to select sounds or music cues at random. A cartridge consists of a loop of tape wound inside a plastic housing (see illustrations 3.4 and 3.5 on page 50). Cue tones are recorded onto a central track that allows the machine to automatically stop at the cue point, fast forward, or trigger

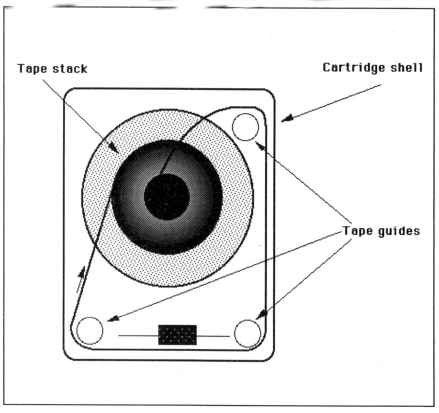

3.4 A plan view of a NAB Cartridge. The tape is pulled from the centre of the reel, passes the playback head and is then wound on to the outside of the spool. Lengths can range from 10 seconds to over 7 minutes.

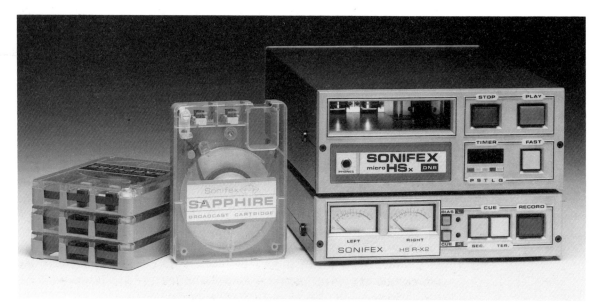

3.5 A NAB cartridge player with associated recorder module.

other machines or effects via a relay closure. These cue tones are known as the primary (stop) tone, the secondary (wind) tone and the tertiary (auxiliary) tone. Once a cue has played, the tape loop simply continues to pass the playback head until the next primary or secondary tone is sensed, then either stops, ready to play the cue again, or fast forwards until either another cue or stop tone is found. In some machines it is possible to disable or erase the stop tone so that the loops play endlessly. This can be useful for long background effects.

Special lubricated tape must be used to avoid problems with friction, and carts are available only in certain fixed lengths, the amount of time available on a cart varies from 15 seconds to over 7 minutes, but it should be born in mind that the only way of resetting a cart to its start is by playing it through at twice the replay speed. A 7 minute long cart that has been started and allowed to play for a few seconds will take around 3 minutes to reset should the need arise.

Cartridge machines replay at speed of 7.5i.p.s.–19cm/s which may be adequate for bandwidth restricted broadcast organisations, but can cause problems in a theatre where an effect may need to be played back at a high level. Noise reduction systems such as Dolby A and SR, dbx and Telecom are therefore often used in conjunction with cart machines to reduce tape hiss.

The best quality cart machines and associated noise reduction systems can cost more than a comparable reel-to-reel machine.

It is best to use one cartridge per effect, but fast sequences may prevent the operator from changing cartridges, so multiple cues may be recorded on a single cart. This can give rise to many problems during technical rehearsals when the operator may have to wind through the following cues each time a section of the play is re-rehearsed. Cost per cartridge is high, so a show using many effects can become expensive; for this reason, theatres using cartridges sometimes keep a stock of carts and re-cycle them as required. Re-loading facilities are offered by some retailers, where the cartridge mechanism is retained, and the old tape replaced with new stock.

Digital cartridge machines

At the time of writing, there are four alternatives to the NAB cart machine in production: the Fidelipac DART, the Sonifex Digicart, 360 systems Discart, and a system from the German manufacturer, EMT. The DART and Sonifex systems both use variations on a 3.5in floppy disk of the type found in most computers, the 360 Systems Discart uses the larger Bernoulli-type disks to store a greater amount of information, whilst the EMT system uses special solid-state cartridges.

These machines can behave exactly like a NAB cart machine, except that all recording and playback is carried out in the digital domain. Some machines can hook up to a larger digital store to access their cues, doing away with the need for a physical cartridge or disk. Cue points and looping are carried out under software control and manufacturers hope to offer extra effects, such as pitch and speed variation.

The recording time available for digital carts using 10 megabyte floppy discs and a sampling rate of 44.1 Khz is in the region of 5 minutes of stereo information. The 360 Systems Digicart is able to store longer sections of audio on the larger Bernoulli- removable disks, but the machine generates quite a high level of physical noise which could be a problem in an open environment.

Because these machines are only just being introduced to the theatre market, there are few reports as to their reliability or with any major problems with the various formats. However, in the UK at least, the Discart and the DART systems seem to have found a number of satisfied users in the theatre world. (See illustration 3.6)

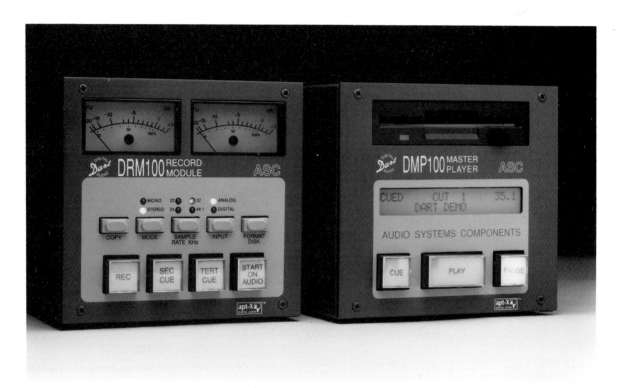

3.6 A digital cartridge player and recorder module.

Digital audio tape   Strictly speaking, digital audio tape can apply to any recording or playback system that stores audio as digital information on magnetic tape. However, the term DAT is widely understood to refer to the system devised by Sony which uses a transport similar to that of a video recorder ie, a record playback head that spins as the tape moves across it. More correctly, we should refer to this system as R-DAT, to distinguish it from other digital systems that do not use rotary heads, such as the Philips DCC (Digital Compact Cassette) format.

R-DAT started life as a consumer format, but failed to take off and was rapidly seized on by the professional recording industry as a low cost digital mastering format to replace the Sony PCM FI system (also originally a domestic format, utilising either the now defunct Betamax video recorder, or more recently, high quality VHS video recorders). Numerical index points similar to compact disc and sophisticated and fast search facilities made the machine attractive to theatre as a device for storage and information retrieval, although research seems to indicate that the useful life of a cassette may not be long enough to ensure that it is a reliable archive medium.

Early machines were robustly built and handled the delicate R-DAT cassette well, but were slow in starting up, with a delay of up to a second before audio was present at the outputs. An attempt was made to modify these machines for a near-instant start, but the procedure was cumbersome, and the conversion expensive. The current generation of machines can have near instant start and the other desirable feature missing from early models, read after write heads for confidence monitoring. With the early machines, you only found out if there was a problem with the recording after you had finished making it. The momentum for using these machines for effects playback during shows seems to have been lost and R-DAT is likely to stay as a means of collecting or mastering material for later transfer to other replay devices. The adoption of a copy prohibit system (SCMS) on domestic and semi-professional machines can also cause problems, but a simple device to defeat the copy prohibit flag is readily available for a small outlay.

DCC is too new to the market at the time of writing to be considered as a serious tool for use in theatre, but as it has been launched almost exclusively to take over from the compact cassette for the domestic market, it is doubtful whether it will find a professional market.

The high end reel-to-reel digital audio recorders made by Studer, Sony, Mitsubishi and others are too costly for playback use in theatre and can be disregarded for the purposes of this book.

Recordable compact disc (CD-R and MiniDisc)

The technology to record one-off compact discs has been around for many years, but only recently has the price become affordable to the average theatre company. In many ways, CD-R is the perfect medium for copying sound effects for a long-running show: the quality of the signal is high, the choice of playback machines is wide, and the medium is reasonably durable, allowing the use of CDs both as a program source and as a convenient means of archiving show tapes.

CD-R systems work by using a layer of heat-sensitive dye between the outer surface and a reflective inner surface. A laser is used to change the transparency of the dye later, corresponding to the digital representation of the input signal. Experiments have shown that it is important to keep CD-R discs away from strong light and heat sources and disc boxes should carry a warning to this effect.

First generation CD-R machines allowed the user to prepare a detailed list of track timings on a computer which could then be written on to the CD as a sub-code, allowing the CD player to display accurate timing information for each track. The newer models do not have this facility as yet, but may well have by the time you read this passage.

Preparing a disc with the latest type of CD-R recorders is simply a matter of lining up the source material, and then hitting the record button on the recording machine at the same time as starting the effect. Once the effect has played through, the machine is stopped and the next effect is added. At this stage, sounds can be added to the disc until it is full, but the disc cannot be played on a conventional CD player. Once the disc is fully loaded with all the required material, any tracks that are not required can be tagged, and a table of contents (TOC) can be generated. The recorder then writes the TOC to the disc, allowing it to be played on a conventional CD player, but preventing any further sounds from being recorded. This process is known as fixing up the disc. If you decide that you want to add an effects at a later stage, then you will have to re-make your original disc, add the extra effects and music, and then re-write the TOC. Blank discs are coming down in price, so this may not be too much of a problem financially, but it can be very time consuming. A new generation of CD players is also coming onto the market that can read a disc that has not been fixed and these are generally professional machines, suitable for use in a theatre.

Equipment exists that will take the output of a Digital Audio Tape (DAT) recorded at the CD mastering standard of 44.1Khz and transfer the contents to CD-R with the index points recorded on the DAT tape being converted to cue points on the CD-R. As there is usually a slight delay between the start of the audio and the presence of the track index on the DAT, high quality digital delays are included to enable the user to ensure that CD-R cue point comes at exactly the right place.

Choice of player is important: cueing from a CD-R requires a specific type of equipment: a CD player that searches for an index point or the start of the audio signal and then goes into pause mode is almost essential. There is an alternative in machines such as those made by TASCAM, Studer and Denon which can be remotely controlled to cue up to a specific time: these machines offer the ultimate in control, but also require sophisticated remote controllers or computer control such as that offered by the McKenzie MIDI Control Program. In general, low-end domestic models will serve for rehearsal purposes, but for performance work, a player that has been designed for continuous operation in a broadcast studio should be first choice. Such machines are invariably expensive, but will last far longer than their domestic counterparts. Computer-based CD Rom players are also being used as a controlled method of playing back audio CD.

MiniDisc   The Sony MiniDisc system has just been launched as a rival to the Philips DCC. The format is a 2in re-writable disc in a small plastic package, capable of storing up to 74 minutes of audio using a data compression system called ATRAC. First reports of this system are encouraging; Sony and Denon have produced low-cost record/replay devices that look and behave like a NAB cart machine. With the ability to add extra cues at any time up to limit of the disc and with sophisticated track identification available, this system must also be considered as a viable option for theatre. (See illustration 3.7)

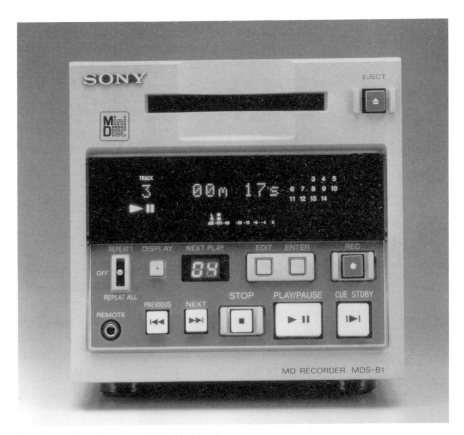

3.7 Sony MiniDisc Record Playback unit.

Hard disk recording systems – stand-alone systems

Of the stand-alone systems available, none are really affordable for theatre record/replay use. Prices are coming down, but this is mainly in response to the personal computer-based systems currently flooding the market. Systems by AMS, DAR, Studer and the now-defunct New England Digital are aimed at high-end recording studio and broadcast users. Their facilities offer much to the theatre sound designer, but at too high a cost to be anything other than a hired-in item for special use. Akai have two products that may be of interest to theatre sound designers. The DD1000 is a four-track record-replay unit, using Sony Magneto-Optical drives for digital storage. The low-cost DR4d and DR8 four and eight track hard disk recorders use a conventional Winchester hard disk, but are less versatile in terms of editing and replay.

At the time of writing, there is a proliferation of digital audio recording cards for personal computers. These range from simple two channel systems with relative crude editing and replay software, up to immensely sophisticated multi-track systems with every editing facility that the designer could wish for. Some theatres have a low-cost version in their dubbing rooms for the preparation of effects and music, but they lack the simple interface and fast start that could make them useful in performance.

A later generation of these machines are being offered to the broadcast industry as a replacement for cart machines: these offer many of the same facilities as the digital cartridge machines, but with access to recorded sounds via a simple remote control and Visual Display Unit (VDU). It is possible that theatre sound designers may see this as an effective way to replace banks of cart machines, although initially costs are bound to be high.

CHOOSING RELAY EQUIPMENT

1) Ease of use

Can the system be operated easily and instinctively under show conditions? Reel-to-reel systems and cartridge machines, both analogue and digital, score heavily here. A few simple controls are all that are needed for operation. Instant or near instant start is easily achieved and each can be operated via a simple remote control. Samplers, compact disc players and R-DAT machines can be more complicated to operate, often requiring complex additional controls and/or computer programmes to function usefully under show conditions.

2) Resistance to failure

How robust is the system? Is it prone to failure under intense operating pressures? Remember that the equipment has to function day after day, very often in a hostile environment. Many pieces of equipment that seem at first sight to be suitable for theatre use, are in fact designed for the domestic hi-fi or semi-professional music market and will not stand up to the sort of use that they will meet in theatres.

Once again, old technology seems to score heavily here. Broadcast standard cartridge machines and recording studio quality tape recorders are built for intensive use. As compact disc becomes the accepted standard for carrying music and sound effects commercially, professional quality CD players are being produced, notably by Tascam, Denon, Studer and Revox. Both samplers and computer-based hard disk/solid state systems can be rendered inoperative by a temporary power failure and require reloading once power is restored. Uninterruptible power supplies can be useful in these circumstances although heat and static electricity can also have a disastrous effect on these systems. Having said that, the author has used Akai samplers extensively with only isolated problems, these being down to operation in high temperature environments.

1 The Birthplace of Scenic Effects

The Paint Room of the Edwin Booth Theater, painted by Charles Witham c.1870. Witham was the chief scenic artist to the famous American actor Edwin Booth.

The artist on the left is working on a backcloth which is stretched onto the wooden frame protruding above it. This paint frame can be winched up and down so that the artist can stand on the floor and work with long handled brushes. (All scenic artists used to wear hats to keep the paint drips out of their hair.)

The picture also shows, on the right, someone cutting a stencil for a repeating pattern, which would be done in much the same way as it is now. The gas batten hanging above the painter will be used for working light when it gets dark. This batten is probably the strongest clue as to the period of the painting.

2 The picture shows a simple yet effective and flexible application of lateral movement technology. The two drapes on the track each have separate linear motor drives at either end. So by remote control the drapes can form any shape from a solid circle to a couple of pillars, and all able to be remotely changed on cue.

3 The doll is fitted with a radio receiver, amplifier and loudspeaker, so that it can 'cry' on cue.

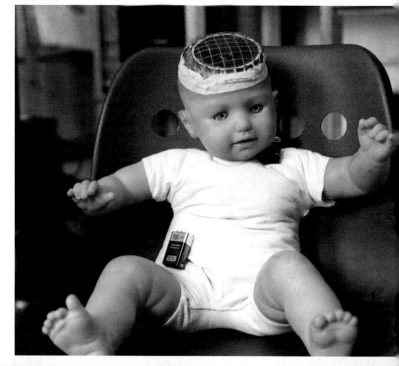

4 One of the earliest examples of composite multiscreen back projections (by converted Kodak Carousels) by Robert Ornbo for *I and Albert* in London 1974, the production was designed by Luciana Arrighi.

5 DHA gobo # 853 projected with split colour filter.

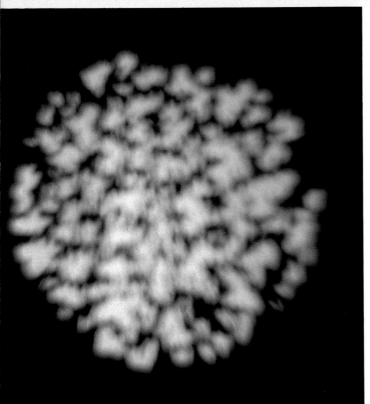

6 DHA gobo # 805 projected out of focus, gobos projected like this with the addition of split colours are more effective.

7 DHA custom made glass gobo.

8 A low voltage light curtain producing intense narrow beams of white light.

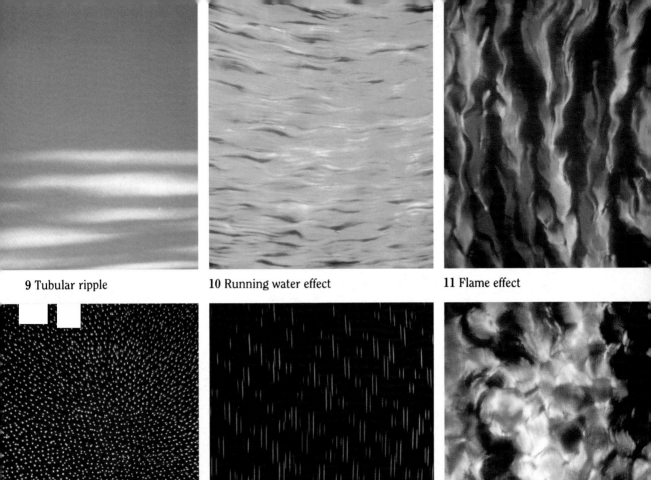

9 Tubular ripple

10 Running water effect

11 Flame effect

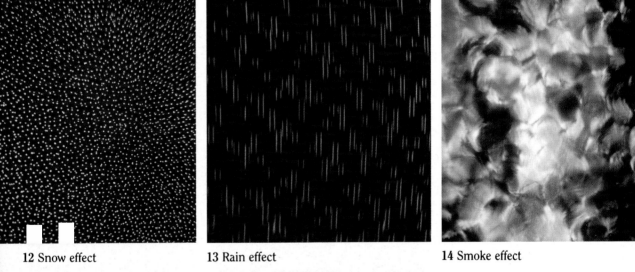

12 Snow effect

13 Rain effect

14 Smoke effect

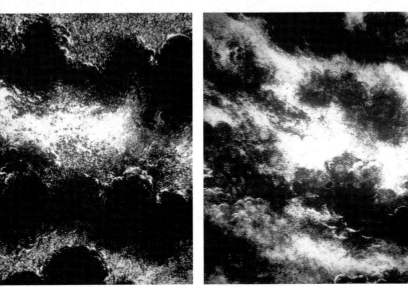

15 Thunder cloud effect

16 Storm cloud effect

9–16 Some of the range of effects produced by the motorised wheels suitable for 2Kw and 2.5Kw effects projectors.

17 *Left*. Overhead projector on a small stage, the projector is concealed behind the centre stage cut-out flat.

18 *Right*. This drive unit can be installed in a piece of scenery or furniture to make it independently mobile via radio control. It has been made from the mechanical parts of a motorised wheelchair, with its joystick linked to the servo control system of a model aircraft. All components barring a couple of pieces of aluminium plate were purchased readymade. The joystick is visible on the left.

19 Herbert Senn and Helen Pond's design (and stunning scene painting) for *Don Pasquale* at the Opera House, Boston, lighting designed by Graham Walne.

20 Impressive projections by world leaders Pani for Siegfried and Roy in Las Vegas.

21 Michael Spencer's simple but effective set for Macbeth for Welsh National Opera, the black wall moves back and forth concealing or revealing characters. Lighting by Graham Walne.

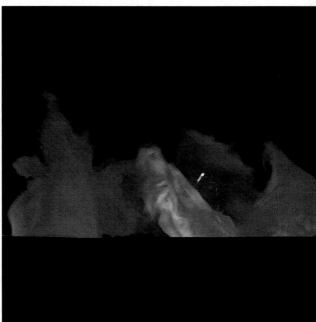

22 *Left*. Side view of a fire machine.

23 *Below*. Silk flames jump 6½ft (2m) into the air.

24 Silk fires leap into the air in the film version of *The Nutcracker* directed by Carol Ballard and designed by Maurice Sendak. Effects design by Jauchem & Meeh.

3) Durability and exchangeability of the medium

Magnetic tape is reasonably durable as a medium, provided certain storage considerations are met. Tapes produced since the 1960s have a binder/base/oxide combination that is largely stable, although problems have been encountered with some brands of tape that have been stored under damp conditions. Remedies, albeit rather drastic ones, do exist for alleviating such problems for long enough to allow a copy to be made. Formats, speeds and track standards for professional tape recorders have been in place for many years now and a common working practice has ensured that it is relatively easy to exchange tapes and be sure that they will work with your equipment. The same cannot be said of the current state of affairs within the digital domain.

Although a common standard is supposed to exist for the R-DAT system of digital recording, numerous cases of machine/cassette incompatibility have been reported. On the exchange of digital audio information between systems, once again, two standards, S/PDIF for consumer equipment and AES/EBU for professional equipment, exist but problems have occurred with a degree of incompatibility being experienced as manufacturers cut corners to save money. When such problems arise in the digital domain, the result is usually a complete failure of the system to replay the stored sound.

The one exception to this is the CD, where the sheer volume of replay product has ensured that standards are adhered to, although I still check my recordable CD masters on the cheapest domestic player, just in case.

Most high-quality samplers will accept sample disks recorded to the AKAI standard, but will not read performance data. The digital cartridge machine manufacturers are also working towards a common standard so that they should be able to read each other's disks.

Playing it back

As well as a way of storing and replaying your sounds, you will need equipment to broadcast them during the play. It is beyond the scope of this section of the book to investigate such equipment fully, but at the very least, you will need a way to combine your effects and music at varying levels ie, a mixing desk, and a means of amplifying the sounds and locating them in the right part of the stage ie, amplifiers and loudspeakers.

There are very few mixing desks built specifically for dealing with sound effects: most theatres use the same desk both for the complex procedure of balancing musicals and for replaying sound effects, with a degree of compromise being inevitable.

The essential elements for any system are the ability to set and vary levels of all the component sounds of your soundtrack, and the ability to determine which loudspeaker or combination of loudspeakers each sound should be sent to. In a large theatre, many loudspeaker locations may be required: the original installation at the Barbican Theatre in London, had provision for twenty-six separate loudspeaker channels, The Royal National Theatre's Main auditorium, the Olivier, had twenty loudspeaker channels when it first opened. The Royal Exchange Theatre in Manchester is currently in the process of commissioning a desk with 20 outputs. It is unlikely that a show will require all of these to be used at once, but a breakdown of the sound requirements of a typical show in a repertory theatre will show that, at minimum, six separate speakers channels should be available.

Tennessee Williams' *A Streetcar Named Desire* is a play with which many readers will be familiar. The script calls for a number of specific effects, some of which are listed:

> the sound of a saxophone playing jazz from down the street
> music from the on-stage radio
> the sound of a shower in the next room
> the clatter of the elevated railroad
> the sound of a distant train whistle
> thunder

Assuming that the director will want music in the auditorium at some point during the evening, we are presented with the following locations. Auditorium (left and right), special for the radio, shower in the next room, street sounds, railroad sounds and thunder. It's possible that the loudspeaker location for the street sounds and the railroad sounds could be the same, but ideally, it would be good to separate them. It would also be useful to incorporate some extra low-frequency loudspeakers, known as subwoofers, to add realism to the thunder and train sequences. Most portable loudspeakers used in theatres are too small to be able to reproduce low frequencies well. The final loudspeaker rig for the show might look like illustration 3.8 opposite.

Locating the loudspeakers

A number of factors other than artistic considerations will dictate where you put the loudspeakers:

Type of theatre: eg, in the round, thrust, proscenium arch, end-stage or traverse.

Set Construction: eg, box-set, open stage, flown scenery, lifts, revolves, trucks, etc.

Aesthetic Considerations: will the appearance of modern loudspeakers seriously compromise the overall look of the piece? (More than one London theatre management insists that luminaires and loudspeakers in front-of-house positions are painted to match the decor of the auditorium.)

Safety: will the actors making a fast exit in a blackout trip over a cable, or bang their heads on one of your loudspeakers? Inevitably, you will not be able to place your loudspeakers where they will do most good ie, directly in sight of the audience! You will have to place them behind flats that are all-too-commonly constructed of solid wood and metal, or amongst mass ranks of luminaires with shutters and colour-frames that rattle and buzz at the slightest provocation, or you will have to fly them to avoid trucks and moving scenery. This is why it is important to have a speaker rig

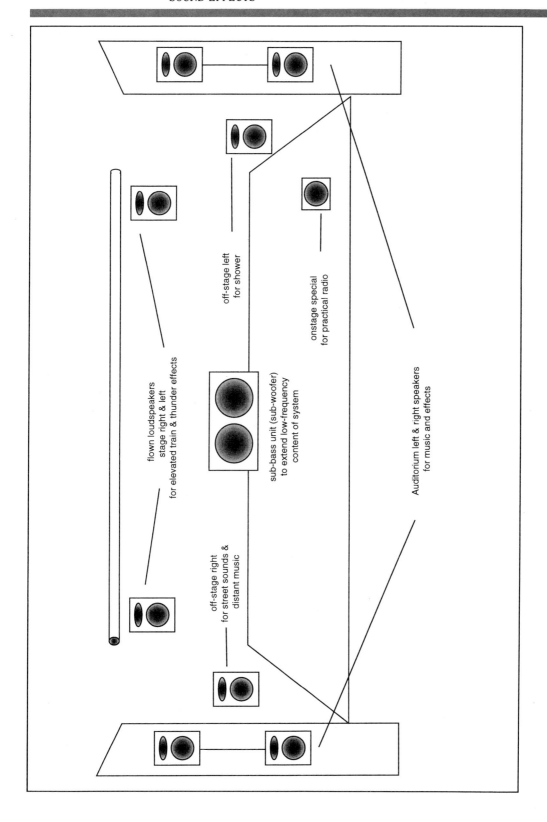

3.8 A theoretical speaker layout for a production of Tennessee Williams' play *A Streetcar Named Desire*.

designed as early as possible, and to get into discussion with the designer and the lighting designer at an early stage. The sooner you declare your problems to them, the more chance you have of reaching a compromise that is favourable to you.

Practicals. Practicals are devices that have to work on stage, such as record-players, tape recorders, radios or televisions. Wherever possible, conceal a speaker in the device and connect it to your sound system so that it is under the control of the operator. If you cannot get a speaker inside the device, then you may try and conceal it on set either above or below the item that is supposed to be practical. If an item has to be moved around the stage, then a number of small speakers can be hidden at varying locations and the signal moved from one to another via the output faders on the mixing desk.

Situations often arise when a practical item is situated on a revolve or on a truck: where there are no slip-rings or cable looms available to feed the signal through, it may be necessary to use a battery operated wireless transmitter/receiver combination of the types used in musicals. The source signal is fed into the microphone input of the transmitter either via a special attenuator lead or a direct-injection box, and the receiver is concealed in the practical, along with a battery powered amplifier and small loudspeaker. I have used this technique with success on numerous occasions, most often to produce a 'crying' baby. The colour illustration 3 shows just such a baby constructed by Philip Clifford, Head of Sound for the Royal Exchange Theatre, Manchester. Similar systems have been used for 'vehicles' that need to move on stage, but use quiet electronic motors. In a production of John Whiting's *Penny For A Song*, a steam-driven fire engine spluttered and gurgled very convincingly with the aid of a small receiver/amplifier combination hidden inside the firebox and a battery operated smoke machine under the funnel to add realism. The Royal National Theatre used the technique for Mr Toad's car in *The Wind In The Willows*, with additional low-frequency reinforcement from a concealed sub-woofer.

Two words of warning: always make sure that you have a back up in the form of a local hard-wired loudspeaker in case the wireless link fails, and NEVER put control of a practical in the hands of an actor. They have enough to concentrate on without having to judge whether they have set the volume of the radio at the right level, or remembered to turn the television back on.

PREPARING THE EFFECTS

Having consulted with the director, composer and other interested parties, it should now be possible to make a schedule of effects and music for use in the show. It is advisable to draw up a cue list ie, a list of sounds against their relative position in the show. If tape, or carts or CDs are being used and the show involves a complex effects and music track, then it will be necessary to apportion the effects to a source machine with regard to timings taken during rehearsals and the results listed on a cue assignment sheet. Finally, as the cues are found or created, a source list showing where they have come from should be prepared. See illustration 3.2 on pages 46–7 for typical cue list and machine assignment sheet.

Paperwork can be tedious, but it will save you time in the long run: the cue list lets the sound designer, the director, the composer and the stage manager all talk the same language; the assignment sheet lets you foresee problem areas and work out how to manage them in advance, and the source list will let you retrieve effects for duplication once you have agreed their use with director. And, if the production is revived in later years, good documentation can make life extremely simple.

WHERE DOES IT ALL COME FROM?

All the above is about preliminary work: necessary, but not fundamentally exciting. How do we actually create the sound effects that we need for a show?

Well, the answer, as is so often the case in theatre: it all depends.

Effects libraries

There is a large number of sound effects libraries available; some are on disk, but the vast majority of these are now available on compact disc. The names of these libraries and the addresses of the suppliers in the UK and the USA are included in the appendix.

Effects libraries are expensive; each disk will cost two or three times the amount that you would expect to pay for an ordinary compact disc, but the price almost always includes the licence to use the effects in a commercial production. Without such a licence, you would be legally bound to seek the permission of the copyright holder each time that you wanted to use an effect, and then to pay a royalty for the privilege. (See the section on music copyright for the current legal position in the UK, page 43.)

The best collections of sound effects CDs (known as libraries) come with a fully cross-referenced index. Computer programmes are available which allow you to search for an effect across a number of libraries that you might own. It is also possible to interface this software to a device called a CD Juke-box and have the program find the effect and play it for you. If you need to mix effects, then you will either need to invest in multiple juke-boxes or use a multi-track tape recorder or a sampler to layer your effects as required. Using such a system can be a fast way to gather together the basic elements for a show, but if you rely on other people's recordings in an unmodified form, then you run the risk of your soundtracks becoming very boring for audience and director alike. Laziness and lack of research in choosing effects can destroy a production for an audience. I have never forgotten the production of *A Streetcar Named Desire*, which was one of my first professional soundtracks: Tennessee Williams writes specific effects into his plays, and the sound of trains passing the ramshackle house features largely in this play. I was restricted in my choice of train recordings from a small library of commercially available recordings, and I spent a great deal of time selecting sounds that did not sound particularly British. I was pleased with the end result, and I thought that I had achieved an atmospheric soundtrack for this play set in New Orleans.

The director was happy and all went well until a few weeks into the run of the play. The show had come down, and I was switching off the equipment when I was called to the stage door to talk to a member of the audience who had asked for the person 'doing the sound effects'. I went down to meet him, glowing with the anticipation that I was about to be congratulated on my work. Instead, I was treated to a longish lecture on the differences between British and American trains. To add insult to injury, he then correctly identified all the recordings that I had thought I had so cleverly disguised. Ever since, I have been almost fanatical about making sure I was as accurate as possible with my sound effects. You never know when you're going to have an expert in the auditorium.

Location recording

In many cases, there is no substitute for getting out and recording the naturalistic effects for yourself. A high quality portable tape recorder, analogue or digital, some microphones with effective wind-shields, a pair of headphones and endless charm will get you a long way in location recording, but first it is essential to make sure that what you are going to record will actually be there when you arrive! I learned long ago that a phone call in advance can save time, money and sanity, but things still go wrong. The recording session for the Sherman tank in *The Desert Air*, was carefully organised with the Tank Museum in Dorset, but shortly before I arrived, a heavy rainstorm deluged the camp, and the tank, with water in the ignition system, resolutely refused to start. Instead I have an excellent recording of a Sherman tank failing to start and a very irate sergeant cursing fluently. Not much use for the show, but it raises a laugh at seminars. In the event, a slowed-down recording of a three ton diesel lorry mixed together with a Caterpillar road mending vehicle did the trick.

Never take permission to record for granted, and always offer to pay a facility fee, even if only a small one. In doing so, you are less likely to alienate the person on whose property you are recording and much more likely to render them friendly for future sessions. By far the biggest problem with recording in exterior locations is that members of the public will come up and talk to you: they will ask you questions just at critical moments, they will shout out their names or call out 'Hallo Mum', or just make silly noises into the microphone. They will think that this is great fun, never dreaming for a second that they have ruined what could have been several weeks worth of planning. There is no real solution to this problem, save that of using concealed microphones or arranging to be in a location to which the general public have no access. Apart from the necessary permission, if you are intending to record on private or public property, you must also make sure that you have public liability insurance. Tripping a member of the public with a microphone cable or dropping a microphone onto a passer-by can be very expensive. The policy will cover you for most eventualities and will not cost you much.

Equipment for location recording

Today, portable equipment is small, light, very high quality and not necessarily expensive. When I first started recording my own effects, I used a Uher portable reel-to-reel recorder and carried around a case full of batteries and small reels of tape. For critical work, I would hire in one of the excellent Nagra portable machines, but that meant even more batteries and, if recording at 15 ips, even more reels of tape. Today I use a portable R-DAT recorder; a larger professional model for critical work, or a tiny pocket model for grabbing effects inconspicuously. Microphones and wind-shields are a different matter. If you are planning to do a lot of your own recording, then you will have to gather together a collection of microphones suitable for all types of recording work.

A high sensitivity microphone that will capture the sound of a mosquito will certainly not be suitable for recording thunder or gunfire at close range. You will need to pick a model suitable for the job that you have in mind and take into account a number of factors which would not normally be a problem. I have yet to come across an all-purpose microphone, although I do use the Soundfield Research ST250 microphone to cover many of my needs. This is a development of the Soundfield microphone from the same company, but with the advantage of being completely portable. The pre-amplifier can be powered by battery, mains, or mixing desk phantom power, and signal output can be designated as an X-Y stereo pair, a Mid-Side pair, or B-Format surround sound. The polar pattern of the microphone is variable, as is the apparent angle between the X-Y capsules, although the microphone actually uses a four-capsule design, deriving its various outputs electronically. The microphone is available with a wind-shield made by Rycote, who are acknowledged experts in this field. The wind-shield is an essential item for exterior recording, as even the slightest breath of wind can register as an annoying low rumble on a sensitive capacitor microphone. (See illustrations 3.9 and 3.10 on page 64.)

Most capacitor microphones and most digital tape recorders are badly affected by condensation: taking such equipment from a cold environment to a warm one can cause instant formation of condensation. Allow time for equipment to acclimatise to different temperatures.

There may not necessarily be a local power supply for you to plug your equipment into, or a pro-audio shop to provide you with batteries, tapes or cassettes. Always take twice as much in the way of consumables as you think you will need.

Sometimes, portable equipment can react adversely to being moved in a particular way: in particular, centrifugal force can play havoc with some rotary head digital audio tape machines, as I discovered to my cost after subjecting myself to a particularly gruelling roller-coaster ride in Disney-land. Most of the recording was perfect, but as the car passed through the part of each turn where the centrifugal force was at its greatest, severe drop-out occurred.

Almost invariably you will have to monitor your recording using head-phones: the open type of headphones favoured by hi-fi enthusiasts may give

3.9 and 3.10 Rycote windshields shown with and without a windjammer outer cover.

superb reproduction, but will be almost useless in a noisy environment. Closed-ear models will give you the acoustic isolation that you need to check if your recordings are OK. If you are recording on to a DAT recorder that does not have confidence monitoring, then be sure to check your entire recording for faults: you may not be able to repeat the session at a later date.

Studio recording

Once effects have been sourced either from a library or from real life, there remains only one other source: the sound designer's own imagination. This is where the real creative work is carried out, first in the mind of the designer, and then in the recording and dubbing studio. A sound effects recording studio should have an area devoted solely to recording acoustically. It should be quiet, reasonably free from reverberation, large enough to accommodate a sufficient number of actors for a convincing crowd scene, and with a variety of surfaces available for recreating footsteps if required. A water supply and a large sink or bath can be a distinct advantage. Few theatres have space devoted to this sort of studio, and rehearsal rooms are often pressed into use as makeshift recording areas. Unfortunately, the poor acoustic properties of these spaces can make them less than ideal unless care is taken to deal with the more undesirable acoustic properties.

The sound effects dubbing studio should contain the means for treating and mixing sound effects and re-recording the result. My own studio currently contains the following equipment:

1 × 1in eight track reel-to-reel tape recorder
2 × high-speed 2 track reel-to-reel tape recorders
2 × R-DAT recorders,
1 × PCM701/F1 stereo digital recording system,
3 × compact disc players,
2 × compact cassette recorders
1 × analog synthesizer
1 × digital synthesizer,
1 × 16 bit digital stereo sampler
2 × MIDI keyboard controllers
1 × computer with MIDI sequencer software and hard disk recording system
1 × 16–4 mixing desk
1 × 6–2 mixing desk
and a variety of miscellaneous processing equipment such as reverb units, noise reduction systems, delay lines, compressor/limiters etc.

In many theatres, the sound-control room also does duty as the dubbing room, but this is a less than ideal arrangement, unless the theatre also has a proper operating position in the auditorium. Even if it is only a small space, all theatres should have a room set aside for preparation of sound effects so that work on a show can take place whilst the control room is in use during performances.

The recording and dubbing studios are the places where technical trickery and personal ingenuity can transform the mundane into the remarkable, mistakes can be rectified and the disparate elements that go to make up a soundtrack can begin the process that will organise them into a coherent whole.

Every studio should have access to a supply of noise-making equipment. This should include at least some of the following types of items:

> bicycle bells, sleigh bells, small hand-bells, wind chimes, door-bells (regular, chime and electronic), tubular bells, alarm clocks
>
> miscellaneous crockery, glassware, cutlery, brooms, saucepans, dustbins (trash-cans)
>
> running water, wash basin, enamel bowl
>
> acoustic piano, side drum, bass drum, assorted Latin percussion, cymbals, finger cymbals
>
> electric fans, motors, mechanical toys, clock mechanisms.

This may look like a formidable list, but you will find that most of the items will either be available to you at home or in the theatre. The secret is to know where you can lay your hand on them quickly! Although many of them will be useful for effects as they stand, all can be pressed into service as a source for other sound effects. In a production of *The Wizard of Oz*, the various clanks and creaks of the Tin Man were produced by mistreating a variety of cooking utensils; kitchen knives and a sharpening steel can prove useful for creating sword and dagger effects; a battery-operated miniature electric drill and a metal ashtray provided a particularly nasty old-fashioned dentist's drill for a Feydeau farce, and two Peter Shaffer plays, *The Royal Hunt of The Sun* and *Equus* have had soundtracks where scraped piano string, bowed and reversed cymbals and a bass drum were used to great effect. In his book on theatre sound, David Collison describes how he and composer Guy Woolfenden created various effects for the Royal Shakespeare Company's production of *Henry V* in 1965, using similar methods.

SOME USEFUL STUDIO TECHNIQUES

Altering the source sound to make it more suitable for use in a production will involve the designer in a variety of processes in the dubbing studio. Some of those techniques are discussed here.

Looping

Many sounds used in plays are of the atmospheric variety and can sometimes be required to play for long periods. If the sound is rhythmical or repetitive in character, the technique of looping, where an endless loop is created, either by joining together the ends of a piece of recording tape, using a tape cartridge or creating a loop in a sampler, can be used to create a long effect from a short one. Care must be taken to match levels so that the end of the loop perfectly matches the beginning. If this is not the case, there will be an audible and disturbing change in the level each time the loop repeats.

Not all effects can be looped successfully: bird-song and animal noises where identifiable patterns repeat are picked up by even the least discerning of audiences if the loop is only a few tens of seconds in duration. Once a loop has become apparent all concentration goes as the listener's subconscious waits for the loop to repeat. Creating long tape loops, particularly when the recording at 15i.p.s.–38cm/s. will involve finding a path for the loop round the dubbing room. Microphone stands and empty tape spools are useful in these circumstances. Human help may also be used, but it can be difficult to maintain the correct tape tension in this case. A microphone stand will remain motionless for hours at a time without becoming bored or restless or needing to visit the bathroom.

A regular crash of waves on the shore is a good sound for looping, provided that the effect is used gently in the background. Wind and rain can both be looped successfully, as can fire effects but longer loops should be used to provide some variation.

Insect sounds are by nature repetitious and short loops can be created with ease. It should be noted, however, that insects do not always sound continuously; the odd quiet passage will add to the verisimilitude of the soundtrack, and the audience will be reminded of the effect each time it restarts after a quiet passage.

Crowd sounds can also be looped successfully, but if the effect is to run for any length of time, a mix of several loops should be used for the sake of variety and reality. The sound of a large crowd waxes and wanes in a fairly random manner: we are all familiar with those occasions in a theatre auditorium before a show starts when the audience suddenly goes quiet for no reason, and then slowly builds up to a more constant sound.

Clocks striking and tolling bells require a more careful approach to looping as the effects normally need a beginning and an end which have to sound natural. The looped chimes must contain an element of ring-on from the previous strike, but the beginning chime must be clean, and the end chime must have a long ring-on to a realistic decay. Ideally, a source effect of three chimes minimum is required for creating convincing clock chimes and tolling bells of any duration. The middle chime is looped, containing as it does the ring-on from the first chime, and the first and last chimes are edited into position after the required length of material has been recorded. A word of warning: you must use a single chime that starts from silence and decays to silence for a clock striking one. Trying to isolate a single chime from the middle of a group, or using the final chime from a sequence, will sound unnatural.

Horse drawn and motor traffic effects will only loop if there are no specific sounds such as shouts, car horns or tyre squeals that will give the loop away to an audience.

Almost any indeterminate atmosphere can be looped, but it is possible to rely too much on loops. I prefer to try and procure long recordings of natural sounds that have their own dynamic, or to artificially re-create sounds with a similar dynamic.

In a recent production of *Heartbreak House*, the director required birdsong throughout a 45 minute scene. During the course of the scene, the lighting state indicated that late afternoon was changing to dusk, then to twilight, then to darkness. Instead of preparing a 45 minute soundtrack of looped birdsong, I used a series of lengthy birdsong effects, gradually thinning them out during the course of the scene, until the only bird to be heard was a distant owl.

The second example involves wind. A similar requirement for a show called for a long wind background: at specific moments, the wind was required to rattle the shutters of the house, or to sound in the chimney. The spot effects were prepared separately and played in as required, but the continuous effect was created using a mix of long naturalistic wind recordings and a synthesised wind, created on an EMS Synthi analog synthesiser. By setting up random pitch variations using the machine's in-built sequencer and two un-synchronised low-frequency oscillators for voltage-to-pitch control, it was possible to create a long wind background in which no mix of elements ever appeared to repeat.

Some effects libraries aid the designer in this respect by providing cuts of atmospheric sounds that are between three and six minutes long. Rather than looping, these may simply be recorded end to end and edited into a continuous track.

Close-up recording

In the same way that extreme close-up photography can reveal unusual aspects of the object being photographed, using a microphone very close to a sound source will reveal many different aspects of even the simplest sounds. When these sounds are amplified a completely different effect may be produced. I needed a swinging inn-sign for a production of *A Tale of Two Cities*, and produced it by recording the creaking sound made by swinging a compact cassette case lid on its hinge. The sound of a crackling fire can be recreated by a close-up recording of the 'bubble-wrap' type of packaging being gently squeezed in the hand, with the odd pop of one of the bubbles adding a great deal to the effect.

In a production of *The Tempest*, we needed a threatening drumming rhythm: nothing that the music department could produce was quite right, but by placing a microphone face down on a table top and then drumming on the table top with finger-tips, the right sound was produced. Feeding the end result through a reverberation unit produced a convincing thunder of drums in the distance. Once again there are no rules: if you think it might work, try it.

Speed variation

Changing the scale of an effect can often be achieved by altering the speed at which it is replayed. A change of speed produces a change of pitch which can alter a sound considerably. A pistol shot can become a cannon shot when slowed down sufficiently. Conversely, a speeded up cannon shot can become a truly remarkable rifle shot when speeded up.

For Peter Whelan's First World War drama, *The Accrington Pals*, we needed a sound that could suggest a massive industrial machine, thumping away in the distance of a small northern town. The same sound had also to suggest distant gunfire on the Western Front. No library effect was suitable, so I used a recording of a spring-loaded date-stamp, thumping down onto a desk. Slowed down to a quarter and then to an eighth of the original speed, and then looped, a satisfyingly sinister and mechanical machine rhythm was created. The slower recording was used mixed with an actual recording of distant gunfire as a background to the battle of sequences in the show.

The digital signal processing devices available today offer two time domain functions not available using analog equipment: pitch variation without speed change and speed change without pitch variation. Used sparingly, these can be helpful to the sound designer. In a production of Jules Feiffer's *Little Murders*, a window is opened and closed at various times by members of the cast. The sound effect that went with the action had all the right ingredients, but was too long: recording the sound into the digital signal processing section of an Akai S1100 sampler allowed me to reduce the playback time without altering the pitch of the effect. Too much variation of either pitch or speed will produce unpleasant distortion, only really useful if you are producing a science fiction sound score.

Echo and reverberation

The use of artificial echo and reverberation to alter the perceived acoustic of a sound has long been a favourite tool of the sound designer. Through the use of digital reverberation and echo units, almost any acoustic condition, whether real or imaginary, can be simulated. The designer should take care at what stage the effect is added, however, as echo or reverberation, once applied to a master recording, cannot be removed without re-making the effect. I prefer to record sounds without processing, adding this during playback in the theatre. If this is not possible, I will prepare twin track recordings, with one track carrying the sound 'dry' and the other treated. That way, the two can be combined in the theatre to give the desired result. Generally, the shorter the reverberation time, the smaller the perceived space: most digital reverb units have controls that allow the user to set the size and shape of the 'room' with a fair degree of accuracy.

In the Royal Shakespeare Company production of *Cyrano de Bergerac*, the play ended with the sound of a distant choir of nuns as Cyrano dies. Our recording session in the theatre early on a Saturday morning was graced by a group of singers who were not in best voice and the resultant recording was not as sweet as we had hoped. The addition of a judicious amount of artificial reverberation coupled with playback from a flown loudspeaker at a very low level produced exactly the effect that was required.

A repeat echo, or slap echo, is often used to heighten battle scenes on stage. Microphones pick up the live action sounds and the signal is then fed to a delay unit set for a repeat time of around a quarter to a third of a second. The delayed sound is then relayed to the stage loudspeakers, where in turn it is picked up by the microphones and fed back to the delay unit. Used subtly, this effect can enhance battle scenes by adding to the general sense of confusion and chaos. Overused, it becomes as much a cliché as too much smoke or dry-ice.

Using reverberation in the same way can help to given an audience a sense of place in productions where there are no visual cues. A small black box can become a cathedral in the mind of an audience if they hear the actors in an acoustic that represents such a space.

Compression

The ear is capable of perceiving a wide range of levels of sound; if this range was to be expressed in a non-logarithmic fashion, the ratio of the quietest sound to the loudest would be around ten million to one. To avoid dealing with such large numbers, we can express noise levels using a logarithmic scale called the decibel (dB) scale, where 0dB sound pressure level (SPL) represents a sound level at the threshold of hearing, and 140dB SPL represents a sound level at the threshold of pain. (This is a much simplified explanation of sound pressure level. For more detail, consult one of the books listed in the bibliography.)

The background level of sound in a theatre can be quite high, certainly reaching levels in excess of 40dB SPL. Sound effects that contain a wide range of levels can easily have their quiet passage lost under the general background noise; a heavy sea effect is a good example. In order to hear the effect during the backwash, the operator increases the level but then the sound of the wave breaking on the shore will be too much and the operator will have to reduce the level once more. In order to avoid this see-sawing of levels, it is advantageous to use a compressor to limit the dynamic range of an effect. The compressor can automatically reduce the higher levels of an effect or piece of music passed through it. Precise settings of the amount of level reduction will depend on the type effect or music. Compression is particularly useful in coping with sounds sourced from digital recordings. (See also **Gunshots and explosions** page 74.)

Equalisation

Equalisers can be used for more than tonal correction: judicious use of a comprehensive equaliser can change the characteristics of a sound so that it is more suitable for a given application. Obvious examples are telephone conversations, transistor radios, public address systems and intercoms. I find that these sounds are enhanced by the use of a distortion box; either a setting in a multi-effects processor or a stand-alone unit as used by rock guitarists, although these can be a little on the harsh side.

Very often, a combination of treatments is required in order to arrive at the correct sound. A modern-dress production of *Timon of Athens* had a scene set at a horse racing track: the sound requirement was for a commentary that should be audible, but not coherent, alongside the sound of thundering hooves in the distance. The race commentator became more and more excited as the scene progressed, but it was important that no actual words should be audible. The answer was to record the commentary and then apply the following treatments:

1) Severe compression so that the voice level was constant. No sudden peaks to get in the way of the text.

2) Drastic application of equalisation to remove all frequencies below 300 Hz and above 3,000 Hz to give that authentic 're-entrant horn' sound.

3) Application of distortion using a Yamaha SPX900 multi-effects processor. Just enough distortion was added to render the words incomprehensible whilst still retaining the sense of urgency.

4) Discrete application of slap echo, with the echo effect being routed to a separate speaker.

The end result was convincing, and distorted enough to ensure that nobody could quite make out that the winning horse was ridden by the director, the second horse by the designer and the third horse by the leading actor.

Composite effects

Rarely will a library effect or a location recording be exactly right for the show. You will have to massage the effect into shape, by using some of the procedures outlined above, but also by editing and mixing effects together. It is often necessary to disassemble a sound and to study the component parts and then build the sound up from scratch. The window opening and closing effect from *Little Murders*, mentioned above, consisted of three sounds: first, the metal against metal creak as the jammed window starts to move, next the sliding sound of the frame in its groove, and finally the sound of the frame hitting the end stop. Finding a library recording that sounded just right was unlikely, so the effect was fabricated. The metal creak came from the noise made by a spool retainer on an elderly Ampex tape machine, the sliding sound was from a greenhouse window, and the bang was taken from a library recording of an old sash window closing. In producing the final effect, it was necessary to 'think' the action of opening and closing the window, and to orchestrate the playing in of the various elements at the correct time.

A colleague, Alastair Goolden, was required to make up the sound of a drink vending machine at very short notice. His analysis of the effect was as follows: coin drops, solenoid clicks, plastic cup drops, pump motor whines, liquid drips into cup, pump stops, solenoid clicks again. He recorded the coin dropping into a metal container, the plastic cup dropping onto a metal tray and the water dribbling into the cup in the dubbing studio, and the solenoid click and pump whine were pulled from the effects library. Most of the component sounds were recorded into a sampler in sequence, having been adjusted for level and length, and then played out as one long effect. The water into the cup sound was mixed in from a separate machine, and allowed to continue for a few drips, after the mechanical sounds had ceased. This was achieved in slightly less than an hour and shows how a familiarity with both process and equipment can help to create convincing effects quickly. The effect was subsequently cut, but this is also something with which the experienced sound designer learns to cope. (The same show used short samples of sound effects in a musical score by composer Jeremy Sams. Set in the foreign exchange dealing room of a merchant bank, the music track was made up from pitched recordings of typewriters, telephones and the bleeps and hums of office equipment.)

For some composite sound effects, it may be desirable to keep the various elements on separate machines for each performance. Timing can change from night to night and the ability to place the different elements in time and space precisely with regard to each performance is very useful. A play by Charles Wood called *Red Star* had a sequence set in a Russian railway station. During the course of the scene, prisoners are loaded onto a train, we hear the doors of the cattle truck in which they are being transported slam shut and the guard call out a warning that the train is about to depart. The train starts to build up steam, a whistle blows, the train begins to move off, sounding its own whistle as it does so. As the train moves out of the station, we hear the whistle again, more distant and finally, we are left in the empty station with the sound of people going about their everyday business. This entire sequence was continuous, and was split up onto three two-track machines in the following way:

> *Deck A track 1* general station atmosphere
> *track 2* stationary steam train; sound of hissing steam and thumping of brake pumps
> *Deck B* truck doors slam shut; followed by
> *Deck C* guard announcement; followed by
> *Deck B track 1* train builds up steam
> *track 2* five seconds of silence then guard blows whistle; followed by
> *Deck C* train moves off – stereo effect with whistle mixed in. Fade out Deck A track 2 under the sound of the train moving off.
> *Deck B* distant whistle.

Each of the tape machine starts were on specific line or movement cues from the actors. The stage was filled with people and props and the cue points varied each night. Trying to create a single effect of the whole sequence would have meant the actors trying to fit their lines and moves to a rigidly defined time scale, with no room for manoeuvre if things went awry on stage.

LIVE EFFECTS

There are some effects that are always better performed live: these can include glass smashes, telephone, door knocks, door bells, small gunshots and controlled explosions.

Glass smashes

It is unusual to see the old-style glass-crash boxes in theatres these days: their place has largely given way to the use of digitally recorded effects. If it seems necessary to use such a box, two alternatives are available: either the use of real glass, in which case great care should be taken in the handling of the effect, with protective clothing and, in particular, eye protection being used; or the use of thin metal plates, suspended on fine nylon wire. The advantage of the second method is that it is much safer, much cheaper and easy to reset. The disadvantage is that it rarely sounds right. In order to get the scale of the effect right, multiple crashes may be necessary along with amplification through the sound system.

Telephones

Whenever possible, the bell or sounder inside the phone should be used. It is usually possible to wire the phone so that the ringer stops as the receiver is lifted. Special telephone ringer boxes can be obtained that will ring the phone in the correct sequence for the country that the action is happening in. There are few stage managers who can recreate and sustain the ringing cycle of the British telephone system manually.

It is also possible to feed audio to the telephone earpiece so that the actor may hear the other half of the conversation if required. If the audience also needs to hear the conversation, the level at the earpiece may have to be so high that it causes the actor discomfort. In this case a local speaker may be used, as close to the actual phone as possible, with a suitably distorted feed from the sound-desk. A second option is to relocate the earpiece to the section of the phone holding the microphone.

The source of the remote voice can either be a recording, although this will need absolutely precise operation if it is not to sound stilted, or an actor with a microphone in an off-stage position. The actor will need to be able to hear what is being said on-stage so a suitable show-relay feed will be required. This method has the advantage that conversations will sound absolutely natural.

Always have a stand-by ringer available, even if this is a simple electric bell in the wings. Plays that use telephone conversations almost always use them crucially to advance the plot and this cannot happen if the phone does not ring!

Door knocks, locks, slams and bells

Most theatres have a device known simply as a 'door-slam'. It usually consists of a full-sized door set into a sturdy, stand-alone frame, and fitted with an assortment of locks, chains and knockers. Actors can create their own effects at the correct point, unlocking and slamming the prop door as required, or a member of the sound or stage-management team can do it for them. Once again, it may be necessary to amplify and treat the sound to give the correct impression of scale. The Porter's scene in *Macbeth* will invariably involve a special session to achieve the correct level and sequence for the knocks which are integrated tightly into the dialogue.

Distant door knocks, slams and creaks will be better as recorded effects, so that there is precise control over the level and location of the effect.

Doorbells and buzzers will most often be live, with the stage-manager or the actor simply pressing the bell-push at the required moment. It is easier for a director to give precise instructions about the length and pattern of any rings to a live operator, than for the sound designer constantly to remake the effect.

It is possible to use a sampler for all these effects, and for the sounds to be triggered by contact closures or pressure pads built in to the set. A number of units exist that allow this to happen using the MIDI interface, and one that will allow the use of wireless microphones to trigger effects remotely, using a small tone generator. Care should be taken that effects played in this way are not subject to spurious triggering.

Gunshots and explosions

These are the most difficult effects to generate from recorded material. They exhibit a dynamic range far in excess of most reproduction equipment, and in the case of explosions, the sudden displacement of large amounts of air is difficult to recreate. Audiences are used to seeing realistic gun-battles and fire-fights in the cinema, where all the sound effects can safely be dubbed on afterwards. Some amusement parks with a cinematic theme also provide recorded effects as part of their live-action sequences, but in these cases, distance helps to mask any obvious lack of synchronisation.

Gunshots on stage as part of the action should, as far as possible, be produced by using a specially altered firearm and blank cartridges. There are obvious exceptions to this: automatic weapons with a high firing rate provide their own problems, as do situations where one actor has to fire a gun in close proximity to another. The flash and debris discharged from the blank cartridge can do severe damage at close quarter. In this case, a gun may be fired in the wings by the stage-manager, or a recorded effect can be used. The wireless MIDI triggering device described above can sometimes be used concealed in a weapon, with the effect being relayed over a local loudspeaker. As with important telephone cues, important gunshots should always be backed up, either with a recorded effect, or with a standby gun in the wings. For really important gunshots, both backup methods should be employed.

Distant explosions can be well served with recorded material. Effects can be created using the speed variation techniques described earlier, or taken from actuality recordings. In the case of distant cannon fire, slowing the effect down to provide a dull rumble is often effective. Close explosions are most often achieved with theatrical maroons, as described on page 116. These have a short, sharp impact that is very effective but has the side effect of making any recorded effects used in conjunction sound as though they are lacking in attack. It may be necessary to reproduce recorded explosions used in this way at a much higher level than might be anticipated.

Trying to record a gunshot, cannon shot or explosion without using compression, will result in a very disappointing sound. If the recording level is set for the initial impact, any reverberation will be almost inaudible and the effect will sound dead and unimpressive. Digital recorders do not overload gracefully and a compressor/limiter is vital to prevent this happening and to compress the dynamic range to something more usable in a theatre.

Fights   Stage fights have to be safe, but to look and sound convincing: no actual contact is made during a fist fight, actors hit themselves to simulate the sound of a punch landing; break-away bottles made of sugar glass or brittle wax are used for bar fights, and chairs and stools are made to collapse easily. Once again, post-dubbed movie fights have led audiences to expect realistic fight sounds and stage fights often involve a great deal of vocalisation to hide the fact that all punches are pulled. At the request of fight director Malcolm Ranson, I arranged a series of 'knaps' (sounds of punches landing) as well as bottle smashes and wood crashes on a sampler, with an operator following the action on stage, for a fight in Michael Bogdanov's production of *The Ginger Man* at the Deutsches Shauspielhaus in Hamburg. Without the sound effects, the fight was pretty terrifying; with the sound effects, it was that degree more convincing. The operator was able to track the fight and spot in the effects by hitting a particular note on a keyboard at exactly the right moment. On the first public performance, the theatre's administrator was so sure that the leading man had received a barstool full in the face during the brawl, that he left the auditorium to go backstage and check that no serious damage had been done.

I have mentioned samplers on a number of occasions throughout this section of the book, so now would seem like a good time to look at their use in theatre in some depth.

SAMPLERS   The advent of digital audio recording technology has changed the way that we can manipulate sound. It is now relatively simple to alter the pitch or speed of a recording, add echo or reverberation, or produce the wide range of familiar effects from the world of modern music. We can also store sound in the same way that computer data is stored ie, on floppy disk, hard disk, or in random access memory (RAM). The near-instantaneous retrieval of data held in RAM can be used to advantage in theatrical productions.

The first system that I used for producing part of a theatre soundtrack was a Fairlight CMI (Computer Musical Instrument). It had a data resolution of 8 bits, came in three large roadboxes and included an experienced operator in the hire price. Composer Ilona Seckacz wanted to use the device to manipulate recordings of a choir and wind, sea and thunder sound effects to form a musical soundtrack base for a production of *Twelfth Night* for the Royal Shakespeare Company in Stratford-Upon-Avon. The ease with which we could access the sounds and replay them from a conventional music keyboard was a pointer to systems in use today.

Today, the technology comes in smaller packages: I currently use an AKAI S3200 sampler that I can carry around under my arm. Control of the unit is via a personal computer that will fit into a briefcase and I use it to produce adaptable soundtracks for most of my shows. Although the memory can only hold six minutes worth of audio at one time, it is possible to connect mass storage devices via the industry-standard Small Computer System Interface, usually abbreviated to SCSI, or 'Scuzzy', so that several hours worth of stereo audio can be stored and either played back direct, or loaded into the memory for later playback in response to a pre-determined program.

In order to see how these devices can be used in theatre productions, we will need to look at how sounds are stored and recalled.

Samplers were originally created to allow a musician to record and replay a sample ie, a short digital recording of a musical instrument, from a synthesizer keyboard. If one note, say middle C was recorded and then manipulated so that it could be played back at a pitch determined by the keyboard, then it would be possible to recreate the sound of a musical instrument without actually having to have the instrument in ones possession. Changing the pitch of a single sample over four octaves did not produce particularly realistic sounds, so a further development produced samplers that were capable of storing one sample for each octave on the keyboard, and later, for even more sophistication, more than one sample per note, the actual sample being played being determined by the speed at which the note was hit. For example, it would be possible to record a note on a piano being played pianissimo, piano, forte and mezzo forte and then to allocate these four samples to the same note on the sampler. A simple program within the sample determines how hard a particular key has been hit and instructs the sampler to replay the correct sound.

This is fine for instruments that have a finite note duration such as percussion instruments, but for instruments that are capable of sustained note length, such as brass, woodwind or strings, a method had to be found to allow for variable note duration as well as variable dynamic. The method most commonly used is to allow the user to select a part of the sampled sound for looping. A sustained note played on a violin will have a beginning, or attack, a period where the note is held, or sustained, and an end, where the bow is lifted from the string. To sustain a note for an indefinite period, the violinist must continually move the bow back and forth on the string, sometimes applying a degree of vibrato with the finger holding down the string being bowed. In a sampler, the operator is given the facility to select a section of the held note for looping, or repeating, until a note-off instruction is received from the device controlling the sampler. The operator may then choose to let the end of the sample play, or to let the sound decay according to another set of parameters.

The operator is also given the ability to change the dynamic of a sample by altering values relating to the attack, sustain, decay and release of an *envelope* superimposed on a sample. For example, an instrument like a piano that normally has a sharp attack followed by a slow decay if the note is left undamped, can be made to have a much slower attack, followed by a very short decay; the sound resulting appearing to have a 'backward' characteristic. Having specified an envelope, further alterations of the sound may be carried out by relating the pitch of the sound to its envelope. A sound that builds slowly from silence, may also gradually increase or decrease in pitch as it does so; similarly, a slow die-away may be accompanied by a slow rise or fall in pitch, depending on how the parameters are set within the sampler. A low frequency oscillator may also be employed to control pitch in a cyclic manner, thus giving the effect of vibrato.

It is also possible to send a particular sound to a specific output of the sampler. Most samplers have multiple outputs so that groups of sounds can appear at specified inputs to a mixing desk: for example, stereo string sounds could appear at outputs one and two, whilst brass and woodwind could be routed to outputs three and four respectively; a lead guitar could output to channel five, bass to channel six, and stereo percussion to seven and eight. Most samplers will allow multiple sets of samples to be played together, restricted only by the number of separate sounds or voices that sampler can produce at any one time. The latest generation of samplers will allow thirty-two sounds to be routed to any of eight outputs at any one time. This may seem more than enough, but in complex musical arrangements, two or more samplers may be required to fulfil the needs of the composer.

There are many other ways in which the sampled sound may be manipulated and subsequently controlled from an external device such as a keyboard, or a music sequencer running alone or on a computer and the final disposition of all the variables available to the operator can be recorded as a program and saved to disk for later recall.

In order to see how this technology is of use to the theatre sound designer, simply replace samples of musical instruments with sampled sound effects. Imagine a musical keyboard with a different sound for each key pressed: twelve different thunder claps spread across the first twelve keys, a continuous rain loop that plays for as long as the key is held down, crickets on another key, and dogs barking and growling on two others. Now imagine that you can spread a whole symphony of wind across the entire keyboard, with a different pitch or speed of wind for each key, and with the aid of a sampler that allows you to layer one program on top of another, you could have a second keyboard to play thunder rain and animals, and yet a third to control the replay of musical sounds! This is exactly the way that many theatre sound designers prepare and replay their soundtracks, using computer programs rather than music keyboards. Some composer/designers generate the music for the show from samplers and produce the entire music and effects soundtrack this way with complex music sequencer packages giving fine control over both music and effects playback.

There is an historical precedent for producing music and effects in this way in a piece of equipment known as the Mellotron. This was a keyboard instrument that used magnetic tape stored in its cabinet. Pressing a key was the equivalent of starting a tape player: a pinch roller and a constantly rotating capstain that ran the length of the machine were held together and the magnetic tape sandwiched in between was pulled past a replay head until the key was released. A spring-loaded pulley then dragged the tape back to the start, ready for the next key press. Typically, each tape held three sounds and a mechanical linkage moved the replay head into a position that determined which of the three sounds were replayed. Initially developed for replacing large string, brass, woodwind or choirs for rock groups on tour, the devices met with much adverse reaction from the Musician's Union and were not widely used.

It is interesting but depressing to note that today, much of the sound of strings, brass, woodwind and percussion that features on music for television, film and popular music emanates from samplers, rather than from live musicians.

The degree of flexibility and control offered by samplers, synthesisers and a vast number of processing devices is made possible by the use of a standard protocol for the transmission of data between them. This is known as the Musical Instrument Digital Interface, or MIDI and, as the name suggests, it was originally developed as a means to allow electronic musical instruments easily to interface with one another. Each note on the musical scale is allocated a unique number from 0 to 127 (or 1 to 128 if the instrument is Japanese in origin). The speed at which the note on a keyboard is hit is also given a value from 0 to 127. So middle C, hit as fast as possible, will have a note-on MIDI value of 60 and a MIDI velocity of 127. MIDI data can be transmitted over sixteen separate channels, with each channel able to carry data relating to the following parameter: note-on, note-off, key velocity, polyphonic key-pressure (sometimes called after-touch), control change, program change and pitch-bend. In addition, the MIDI standard allows for the transmission of time data (MIDI Time Code) and data relating specifically to a particular manufacturer (System Exclusive).

Other items that can come under MIDI control include signal processing devices such as reverberation and echo units, graphic equalisers, digital delays, audio patch bays and digital attenuators. In fact, most items of professional audio equipment that have user-variable controls now offer remote variation of some if not all of those controls via a MIDI interface. The list now includes some theatre lighting boards and accessories as well. What started as a means of communication between synthesisers has now matured into a useful means of complete system control.

Hardware devices exist to allow channelling of MIDI information from a computer music sequencer through extra MIDI ports, allowing over one hundred separate MIDI channels to be addressed at once, software and computer power permitting. Additional devices are available to allow MIDI control of non-MIDI replay machines such as compact disc players, tape machines, laser disc players and video recorders.

COMPUTERS AND MIDI

Triggering of samples, control of other hardware and altering system parameters via MIDI used to be a complex matter involving several different controllers, devices for merging the MIDI data and a tangle of cables and interface boxes. With the continuing development of MIDI-related computer software, it has become possible for most functions to be controlled from within one computer program.

The normal method of transmitting MIDI data for use in musical applications is via a music keyboard controller or a computer program known as a sequencer. It is possible to utilise these devices for theatre applications but the interface between operator and controller can often be intimidating and unnecessarily complex. A number of manufacturers have produced programs for originating and manipulating MIDI data specifically for theatre applications and these are available on a variety of computing platforms. I shall examine three such programs in the following sections and although these are by no means the only programs available, they should give the user an idea of how different types of programs can be used in theatre effects work.

One program, Vision™, by OPCODE Systems, for the Apple Macintosh™ range of computers is sold mainly as a high quality music sequencer package, but has been adopted by a number of sound designers in the UK as a show controller. (In the USA a system using the MIDI programming language MAX called LCS is in use on a number of shows.)

A version of Vision™, called Studio Vision™, enables the user to incorporate sounds digitally recorded on a computer hard disk using the Digidesign Sound Tools system, into the MIDI environment. A similar system is available for the Amiga range of computers, using a program called Bars and Pipes Pro™ by Blue Ribbon Soundworks, as the computer sequencer, and the SunRize™ Digital AD516 hard disk digital recording system. In both cases, tracks recorded on the hard disk systems are available to the music sequencer as 'virtual' tracks, and the computer will lock the digitally recorded sound in synchronisation with the MIDI data recorded on other tracks. Using hard disk recording boards and a fast computer, it should be possible to produce a complete music and effects work station, with long audio tracks being pulled direct from hard disk, whilst MIDI events are handled by the sequencer program. The secret of a successful theatre sound work station such as this will be the front-end or user interface: if this is not sufficiently clear and accessible, then time may well be lost in technical rehearsals whilst the operator waits for slow screen updates, or data management.

Vision™ for the Macintosh™

Of the three systems considered here, the Macintosh-based Vision is probably the most intimidating to the untrained user, with a complex screen display and a labyrinthine menu structure compared to the other two systems. However, it is an extremely detailed program, aimed squarely at composers wishing to produce elaborate musical arrangements. Triggering sequences of events involves typing a key command from the computer keyboard which means that the operator must have access to the keyboard during the show. The program has help screens available so that the user does not continually have to refer to the manual.

This system has the advantage of being very easy to integrate with music that has been composed using synthesisers and samplers. In this case, the control of music and sound effects from within the same program can help to smooth the path of technical rehearsals. A piano-roll type graphic display

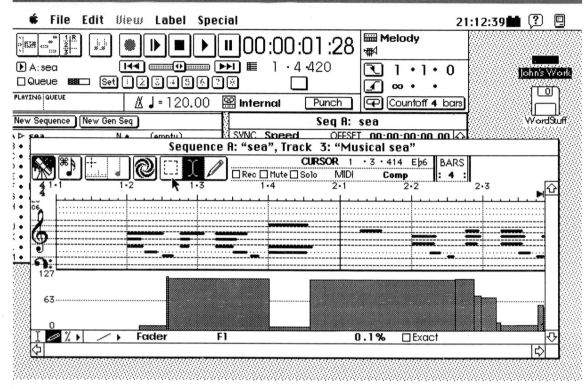

3.11 The sequence editing page for Vision.

3.12 The main display for OPCODE Systems VISION program for Apple Macintosh range of computers, showing the use of music-style sequences to trigger sound effects sequences – in this case for Paul Arditti's acclaimed sound-score for Arnold Wesker's play *Kitchen*, at the Royal Court Theatre.

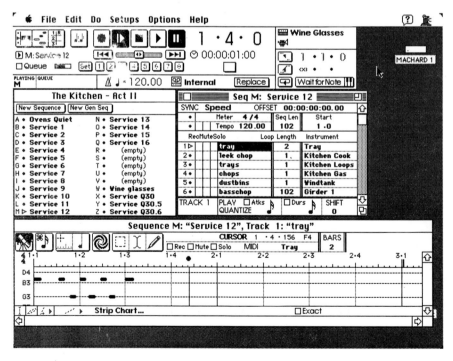

of MIDI sequences (see illustrations 3.11 top left and 3.12 bottom right) enables the composer/sound designer to effect quick alterations to a sequence using the on-screen tools without having to invoke a separate section of the program and with the option of saving the changes, or discarding them. The multitude of options available to the music composer in this program may not be of use to the designer of a simple show, but some form of control over every aspect of standard MIDI functions is available for the power user.

The latest version of this program (Version 2) has a much improved screen display – this, coupled with the faster Macintosh computers now available may help to increase the use of this program in theatre.

Richmond Sound Design Stage Manager® for the Amiga

The Commodore Amiga-based Richmond Sound Design Stage Manager® programs are written with show control in mind and use the custom video chips inside the computer to handle screen updating. They present a very simple screen to the operator, with more complex screens available for editing and modifying data. Stage Manager is also able to take advantage of the multi-tasking operating system of the Amiga to allow the user to run other programmes at the same time, and can also interface with music sequencer programs and hard disk-based recording and replay systems if required. Triggering of events is via a purpose built remote, or the computer keyboard. No help screens are used, but program commands are well laid out and defined.

Multiple cue lists may be run simultaneously, triggered either manually, in response to an internal clock, in response to an external time-code source, in real time, or in response to MIDI Show Control commands. Each cue-list can be controlled differently, and inter-list control is also possible. The program also offers control of external devices that respond to MIDI Machine Control and MIDI Show Control, as well as devices that can be controlled by RS232 or 422 serial instructions with the use of an external interface. An additional module allows the control of suitable CD-ROM players as an audio source, capable of frame-accurate location of cues. Using multiple controller cards, it is possible to control 24 separate CD-ROM players, each with a separate cue list under the control of the computer. (See illustrations 3.13, 3.14, 3.15, 3.16, 3.17 on pages 82–3.)

It is possible to link two computers together via MIDI and to allow the second machine to track the first for backup purposes. The complexity and stability of this program make it the choice of many theme parks and exhibitions in the USA, Europe and Japan, as well as many theatre companies throughout the world. A separate hardware package, Command/Cue™ is available to allow complete control of lighting, sound, servo-motors, hydraulics, contact closures and many other effects devices.

MCP for the IBM PC

Matt McKenzie's MIDI Control Program (MCP) is written for the IBM PC-clone range of computers and has a screen display based on modules that can be added or removed as required. As all information relevant to a cue or

Five screens from Richmond Sound Designs Stage Manager 3000 program showing 3.13 multiple cue-lists open and the control panel for MCD-MIDI Show Control of CD-ROM based playback devices; 3.14 the MIDI sequence editor in which complex MIDI cues can be created and altered; 3.15 the MIDI Show Control page, MSC messages can be prepared for communication to other MSC Devices; 3.16 the RS232/422 page, where messages can be prepared for devices that respond to serial control; and 3.17 the cue list page, where cues can be deleted, loaded to the edit page, or loaded to standby. This complex program has many more aspects: a detailed description can be found in John Huntingdon's book *Control Systems in Live Entertainment*.

3.13

3.14

MIDI SHOW CONTROL Editor

Device ID	All Call
Command Format	Audio Effects Devs.
Command	TIMED GO

SEND   USE   CANCEL

EDIT DATA

type 31 CM +hr mn sc fr ff

Cue Number		Opt	CLR▼
Cue List		Opt	CLR▼
Cue Path		Opt	CLR▼

3.15

Richmond Sound Design Sysex Editor

MTS-232 Messages

SEND   USE   CANCEL

Device #	30
Chan #	4
RTS/DTR	On
PARITY	Even
Send Data	Hex	Asc

3.16

LIST

LIST   3   Work:Richmond/Shows.old/Cues

CUE NUMBER	DESCRIPTION		LOOP	TIME
1.	Crowd murmur Cue 1 S1 & 2	¼	x000	PRESS F10
2.	X fade crowd. 1&2 out 3,4,6 up	½	x000	PRESS F10
2.1.	New Crowd builds 3,4,6.	½	x000	00:00:00:10.0
3.	Crowd for Caesar SL Ch.5	¼	x000	PRESS F10
6.	All crowd out (Ch 3 only.)	½	x000	PRESS F10
7.	Cheer 1	~	x000	PRESS F10
8.	Pulse intro Ch. 1 & 2	¼	x000	PRESS F10
9.	Cheer 2	~	x000	PRESS F10
10.	Cheer 3	~	x000	PRESS F10
11.	Stop pulse Ch. 1 & 2	¼	x000	PRESS F10
12.	Go Pulse 2 Ch. 1 & 2	½	x000	PRESS F10
13.	Music sting Ch. 3 & 4	½	x000	PRESS F10
14.	Thunder & pulse out. Ch. 7 & 8	~	x000	PRESS F10

Load to STANDBY   Load to EDIT   Delete   Print

| | Total | Used | Available |
| | 500 | 113 | 387 |

3.17

sequence of cues is displayed on screen at the same time, there is no problem about screen updates.

The program incorporates a number of special commands that allow the control of a number of non-MIDI devices such as NAB and digital cartridge machines, tape recorders and compact disc players, and in the case of the Denon and Tascam pro CD players, frame-accurate location of cue points can be achieved. Movement around the modules is effected via the computer keyboard, with event triggering being via purpose built remote, or keyboard commands.

Help screens are available for each part of the program and the visual interface can be customised by the user. A novel feature is the ability to open a window that will display a video signal, such as the feed from a closed-circuit TV camera, connected to a suitable interface card.

The program was originally written for Autograph Sound Recording Ltd., in London, to allow complex control of MIDI events in conjunction with VCA control of mixing desks produced by Clive Green's CADAC company, but is also available as a stand-alone program. (See illustration 3.18)

Users of Atari computers may wonder why I have not included their excellent machines. This is simply because I know of no commercially available *theatre* based software for the Atari range.

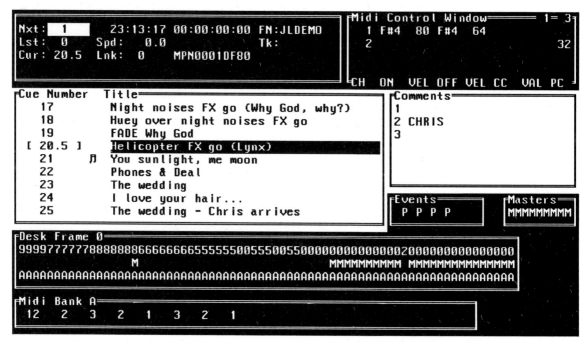

3.18 The main screen of Matt MacKenzie's MCP program for IBM-PC Compatible computers, showing control windows for CADAC VCA system, contact closure event switching, and additional comments along with MIDI information.

PUTTING TOGETHER A SOUNDTRACK USING SAMPLERS

Using a sampler for creating and reproducing sound effects requires a very different way of working from conventional methods: first it is necessary to prepare and load the raw material into the sampler. Given that the sampler's memory is limited, the material must be saved to an alternative storage medium, either floppy disks, or a mass storage device, such as a Winchester-type hard disk, either fixed or removable, or a magneto-optical hard disk cartridge. The mass storage devices are preferable to floppies, simply because access time is much faster, and large amounts of data can be stored on one drive.

Different samplers use different conventions for recording samples, but in general you will be able to choose the sampling rate at which you record, how much space you want the sample to occupy, expressed as minutes and seconds and to set the recording level for the incoming signal. High quality samples will take up a great deal of memory and disk space, so care is needed in deciding what to sample. As a rough guide, one minute of audio at the sampling rate of 44.1Khz will occupy 5 Megabytes of disk space. Such a sample is too long to fit on a floppy disk, and must be stored on a hard disk. For stereo samples, it is necessary to double the storage space requirements.

Most samplers provide useful tools to allow samples to occupy a smaller amount of space than would normally be the case. It is possible to define a loop within a sample so that it will repeat until a note-off command is received. In the case of a tolling bell, or a background of crickets, for example, it is only necessary to record a short section of the sound, and then to instruct the sampler to loop between a pair of defined points. Multiple loops are also available, so that a section of a sound may be looped for a certain length of time, then a further loop may be defined between a second pair of loop points, then a third, and a fourth until the limit is reached. Thus, a short thunder rumble may be turned into a much longer one, by defining multiple loop points within the original sample.

Time stretch and compression functions are included as well as the ability to mix two samples together to form a third, or to join two samples end to end, with user-determined start and stop points.

Once all samples have been prepared, identified and stored, then the next part of the procedure can start. This involves preparing a program which will contain a number of keygroups. A keygroup can consist of a single note or a group of notes on a notional keyboard to which an individual sample, or group of samples can be assigned. This may sound complicated, but it is quite easy to understand in practice.

For example, a keygroup is created, and assigned to the note middle C, or MIDI note 60. It is then possible to assign a sample to this note, say a pistol-shot. Anytime the note middle C is played on a keyboard connected to the sampler via MIDI, the sampler will play the sound of a pistol shot. More than one sample can be assigned to a note, either to play at the same time, or at different key velocities eg, a quiet thunder rumble might be assigned to MIDI note 24 to be played at a key velocity of 0–32. A second, louder clap can be assigned to the same note, to be played at a key velocity of 31–62. A third and still louder clap for key velocities between 63 and 94, and a final cataclysmic clap at velocities from 95–127. If the key is struck gently, then the first clap will play, if slightly faster, then the second, is faster still, then the third, and at the fastest, the fourth clap. Many variations on this theme are possible, with samples overlapping for complex layering of sounds. Attempting to control this from an actual musical instrument keyboard would require the skill and dexterity of a concert pianist, which is why the MIDI control programs are so vital to the use of samplers in theatre sound.

Each MIDI note can have a sample or group of samples assigned to it, giving a total number of 128 different effects per MIDI channel. More programs may then be constructed with different keygroups using different sound effects, up to the limit of the sampler. In the case of the AKAI S1100, this is 99 programs. Using the MIDI program change command, it is then possible to select a new program and therefore a new set of effects, from either a keyboard, or computer controller.

If a keygroup is created and assigned to more than one note, then it is possible to vary the pitch of the sample depending on which note is pressed, thus creating instant pitch variations of the original sound. It is possible to modify the way that a sample is played back from within a keygroup; pitch and loudness may be altered, a filter may be employed and the envelope of the sound may be altered ie, the way the sound begins, decays and ends, so that a sample that has an abrupt start may be tailored to slowly fade in.

It is also possible to apply pitch variations depending on a second envelope generator: setting a long slow attack and a long slow release and then applying this envelope to the pitch of the sample can result in a slow increase in pitch as the note-on command is given, followed by a slow decrease when the note is released.

An example of utilising looping, envelope alteration and pitch variation via envelope, was the use of a multi-sample for the sound of an airship in Shaw's play *Heartbreak House*. The airship sound consisted of a short sample of an aircraft engine, slowed down, and mixed with a sample of two cellos playing a low drone. The pitch of the cellos was matched to the pitch of the aircraft engine, and then looped within the sampler. All elements were kept as separate samples, but assigned to the same keygroup so that relative levels could be altered as required. During the course of the action, the airship has to start and stop its engines, so a decrease in pitch and level was required for stopping the engines, and an increase in pitch and level for the start-up. A loop was established for the drone, so that only a short sample was needed in the memory. An envelope with a slow attack and long release was programmed so that the drone would slowly increase in volume at the note on message, and then decrease in level when the note-off command was received. A second envelope, controlling the pitch of the drone was also programmed, also with a long attack and decay. As the envelope ramped up, so the pitch of the drone increased, until, as the note was held, it reached a steady volume, and a steady pitch. When the note was released, the pitch slowly fell, as did the volume. Similar methods may be used to simulate the effect of police sirens approaching and passing, or any form of machinery starting up or slowing down.

A keygroup may also contain information about how the sample should be replayed: whether the loop points set at the recording stage should be ignored, or if the loop should continue until the note-off command is given, or to continue during the decay time set for the sample envelope. Although this facility was intended for musical purposes, it can be extremely useful in effects work.

EXAMPLE

In *Othello*, an alarm bell is rung after a fight between Cassio and Montano; Othello enters and, some lines later, says the line 'Silence that dreadful bell . . .'. If the bell is on tape, the operator has to make sure that the fade-out between chimes is clean, so that the natural die-away of the bell is preserved. This invariably sounds false, as the final die-away should always be much longer than the gap between chimes, but if the effect is of a fixed length, there is always the possibility that something may occur to lengthen the action, in which case Othello's line may well be said in silence. The sampler gives an easy solution to this: a sample is recorded of a bell tolling three times, with a natural start and end. A loop of the middle bell chime is programmed, and the sampler is instructed to play the sample, looping the middle chime until the note-off command is received. At that point, the remaining part of the sample ie, the natural decay of the last chime, is played. Thus the effect has a natural beginning, a middle section that is as long as is required, and a natural dying away.

Most samplers have more than one output. The most basic stereo sampler has two outputs, and the more advanced samplers have eight or, in the case of an expanded S1100, sixteen outputs. Each sample can be assigned to an individual output, giving immense flexibility for replay purposes. The sampler can be thought of as providing eight mono sources, four stereo sources, or one eight-track source, or any combination in between. These combinations can change from cue to cue and the sampler can also be used as a music source, if required. See illustration 3.19 on page 88 for a typical MIDI relay set-up.

To use a sampler successfully, the designer must have a thorough working knowledge of MIDI, as well as being conversant with the workings of the sampler and control program being used. Instruction manuals for these devices are often aimed at the non-technical user and can often omit useful information. If the designer is unfamiliar with the equipment, then acclimatisation should be allowed for in the pre-production period.

CUEING

The cue light system is explained fully in Chapter 6, page 133, but in some theatres no cues are given during the performance. The operator is expected to follow the script and to take his or her own cues. The stage manager may warn the operator of large blocks of cues, but even this is omitted in some theatres. In many ways, this is a satisfactory arrangement as it involves the

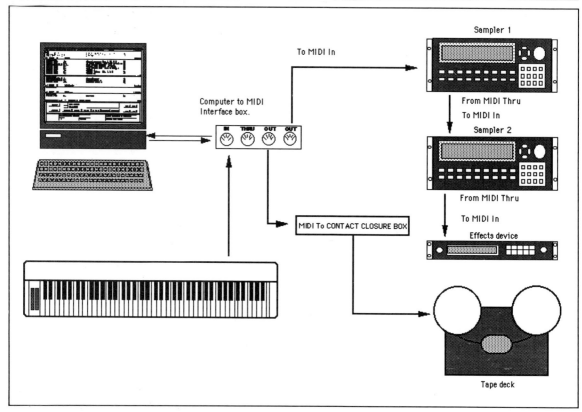

3.19 A typical MIDI effects replay set-up. The tape deck may be replaced by any device that relies on contact closure for start/stop operations. It is also possible to control many other devices using MIDI Machine Control or MIDI Show Control systems.

operator in the production in a positive way, but there can be occasions when it is essential that effects are cued by the stage manager as they may be affected by situations that only the stage manager can see.

Intercom systems are relied on in situations where it is necessary for the stage manager to identify particular cues or actions to the effects operators, or where it is essential for the operator to be able to respond verbally to the stage manager. For a sound operator, this can be restricting as it usually requires the wearing of a headset. A convenient compromise can be reached by using cue-lights until it becomes necessary for voice communication, at which point a flashing light on the intercom unit can attract the attention of the operator.

OPERATING POSITIONS

It is odd that so many theatres spend large sums of money on buying and installing state-of-the-art sound equipment, and then position the operator in a sound-proof booth where, if the live performance can be heard at all, accurate perception of the balance of a sound track is impossible. Mostly,

25 The Temple of Solomon burns in Verdi's *Nabucco* New York City Opera.

26 A large flashpot announces the entrance of the Dragon in the American Premiere of Glinka's opera *Ruslan and Ludmilla*, scenery by Herbert Senn and Helen Pond. Effects design by Esquire Jauchem.

27 A locking pyro control panel with 'arm' switches and indicator lights.

28–29 *Right and below*. The Nabucco declares himself God and places the crown on his head and is engulfed in lighting.

30 A lighting bolt arcs from the sky to hit the king in *Nabucco*.

31 During the storm in *Otello*, a lightning bolt strikes the middle of the stage in a 5000 seat wrap round arena production. Effects design by Jauchem & Meeh.

32 With a star drop to the rear, an illuminated moon floats slowly across the stage among the dancers in a production designed by Robert Wilson.

33 Cooled glycol fog creeps onstage around the Prince in *The Nutcracker* film.

34 PVC drainpipe with holes drilled every six inches is used to deliver fog along the groundrow.

35 A yellow cloud is produced by a 'smoke cookie' burning in a bowl, held aloft by an actor.

36 Dry ice fog fills the graveyard in *Der Vampyr*. Effects design by Esquire Jauchem.

37 Battery powered mice with LED eyes were created for Maurice Sendak's *The Nutcracker*.

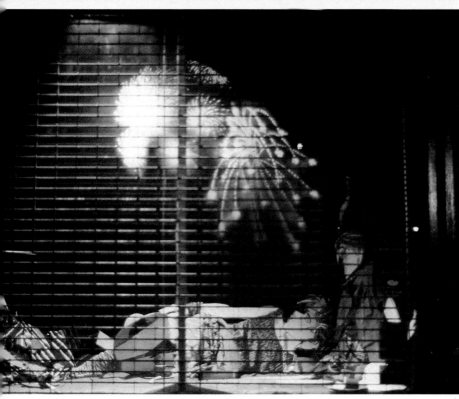

38 A stylised burning cross is created with neon in Michael Tippet's Opera *The Icebreak*. Effects design by Herbert Senn and Helen Pond.

39 Rear projection fireworks illuminate a department store window.

40 Electronic fireworks light up the sky in a touring production of *Gigi*. Effects design by Gregory Meeh.

41 A Prompt Desk
All cues to all departments involved in an effect are signalled from the prompt corner. The essential features of a desk are:
- a clean surface for the prompt book to rest on
- microphone (right) with selector switches to zones being addressed
- cue station stand by and go switches and indicators (centre), each pair controls red/green lights at a specific location
- the single green switch at right is for giving multiple simultaneous 'go' signals
- the white centre strip allows the locations of the cue stations to be marked
- intercom control for the personal headsets of crew/personnel (bottom left)
- clock and stopwatch (top centre)
- effects control switches (left centre).

this is due to the physical size of mixing consoles, but even when new theatres are planned and built, the sound position is confined to a glassed-in booth in the rear wall of the house. There seems to be a feeling that it is only necessary for the operator to be able to hear in the case of a musical, although why this should be so, I cannot imagine.

It is essential for a sound operator to be able to judge, accurately whether a particular effect is being played at the correct level, and the only way that can be achieved is for the operator to be in the same acoustic as the audience. Architects and theatre consultants who think otherwise should consider the cost involved in building the 'soundproof' booth of which they seem to be fond, against the fact that most sound operators and the sound designers will spend their lives in the theatre looking for ways to avoid using these rooms. By all means, build a control room, but please also allow for an operating position in the body of the house. More importantly, let this be an area that cannot be used for audience seating: once the space is lost to a paying customer, it will be very difficult to recover it for its intended use.

ENDPIECE

Sound is subjective: each person hears and reacts to sound in a different way. It follows, therefore, that what sounds right to you will not necessarily sound right to your director or your audience. What works and what doesn't can only really be discovered by trial and error: I have spent many hours on creating complex effects in the studio, only to discover that they failed to work satisfactorily in performance. When this happens, there is no option but to start again. It is all too easy to get carried away in the creation of extremely complex effects that are lost on an audience who are concentrating on the action of the play; in this case, simplifying the sound can make it less distracting for the audience and therefore more effective.

EXAMPLES

Shaw's *Misalliance* requires a light aeroplane to circle the stage, then crash land in the (off-stage) greenhouse.

Bearing in mind that this play was written before the advent of electrical effects reproduction in theatres, this sequence must have been a tall order for the sound effects man! I have worked on two productions of this play, with radically different approaches to this section.

The first, at the Bristol Old Vic, was very simply achieved. The aeroplane sound-effect (a slightly modified library recording) was slowly faded in on a flown backstage speaker placed upstage right, then cross-faded to a second speaker in the body of the auditorium on the stage right side. By this time, the actors were following it with pointing fingers, and the sound operator cross-faded the effect to a second auditorium speaker, this time on the stage left side, following the actions of the actors. A further cross-fade to a speaker at downstage left completed the plane's circular flight path, and the operator cut the 'engine' effect, and snapped in a composite effect of glass breaking, wood snapping and general mayhem. A prop wheel was rolled on to the stage, and a short time later, the Aviator appeared. The action is commented on almost continuously by the actors on stage, so there is no real need for the audience to see what is happening: the combination of the description and the sound effect serves to give the audience a mental picture of the sequence of events. The effect was simple to achieve, and almost inevitably produced, as was intended, laughter.

The second production, many years later, was at a much larger theatre with a much larger budget. The director had decided that the audience should see the aeroplane approaching, and that a full-sized plane should actually crash into the on-stage conservatory. The first image of the plane would be projected onto a back-projection screen, then a small-scale model would appear, to be replaced at the critical moment with the full-sized model on an articulated arm. The actress playing the Aviator was required to jump out of the model at the last minute in an acrobatic fall, leaving the unmanned aeroplane to crash spectacularly into the conservatory. Because the aeroplane was to be visible throughout the sequence, the recorded sounds had to match the visuals, and, as it was by no means certain how long each stage would take until we had rehearsed the effect several times, it was necessary to prepare a complex soundtrack with different effects to match the different visuals. In addition, the director wanted to hear the engine of the plane splutter and cut out just before it crashlanded.

I contacted a pilot with an elderly light aircraft and arranged to carry out location recordings of the plane circling and approaching. When I arrived to do the recording and we discussed what was needed, the pilot readily agreed to carry out all that I asked, and suggested that he should simply turn off the fuel to the engine during the circling flight, then, once the engine had cut out, he would go into a steep dive, restore the fuel supply, re-start the engine, recover from the dive and land safely. He seemed confident that he could do all of this without difficulty, and proceeded to produce a set of excellent effects for me to record, including the alarming sounds of the engine mis-firing and the steep, un-powered dive, with the air rushing through the supporting wires.

I prepared the effect using four separate machines. The first track contained just a simple recording of the plane circling at a distance, the second track was the approach, still under power, the third track was the engine trouble effect, and the fourth a shortened effect of the un-powered dive. The first and second machines having played out their first effects, were cued up to provide the sound of the aircraft crashing into the conservatory: a mix, much as before, with mainly glass and wood breaking. As the visual effects were to be concentrated in one place, I used only three locations for loudspeakers: flown upstage right, flown and floor level in the area that the model and full-sized planes appeared, which was mid-stage right, and finally in and round the conservatory, mid-stage left. The operator was able to cross-fade between them as required, and to re-route tape machines to different outputs with a computer-assisted switch matrix.

When I played the complete sequence in the theatre for the first time, without the film or the models, it earned a spontaneous round of applause from the technical crew and it was, for me, the only time that the effect ever worked satisfactorily. The addition of the film, the model, the full size replica and the safety considerations for the actress, slowed the whole sequence down to a point where it no longer became believable to the audience. It became an effect purely for the sake of being an effect and took up enormous amounts of rehearsal time. By keeping all the separate elements on different machines, we were able to track the timing of the action in case of problems with one section or another of the sequence, with the various effects only being played in as the relevant on-stage action was completed. In performance, the effect worked tolerably well, but the audience was left to imagine nothing and although the whole effect sometimes won applause, it was applause for the execution of the effect, not for its relevance to the production.

4 Lighting Effects

GRAHAM WALNE

PREPARATION

The most important aspect in preparing effects is to recognise the time that must be allowed in which to conceive, realise and rehearse them. Most effects require some degree of manufacture; slides and gobos for example will take at least ten days and probably more if special glass is required. This does not include the time which will be needed to prepare the artwork or collect the visual material from which the gobos or slides will be made. Almost invariably the projectors will not be owned by the company mounting the production because they are expensive to buy and so it is cheaper to rent. This means that quotations must be sought from hire companies, and availability of equipment must be checked well in advance. The costs must be fed into the budgeting system, scenic projection in particular has a minimum cost relating to its process and thus if scenic projection is planned then it is wise to look into this before the budget is fixed. The costs of projections are high but can often be cheaper than the equivalent scenery they are representing or replacing.

There is a tendency to assume projections (and lighting) can solve problems which arise in other departments and many a lighting designer has been engaged late in the day and then faced with a fait accompli which is virtually impossible to resolve because of inadequate time, space or resources. It is vital that the effects expert, in whatever field he or she might be, should be consulted the moment that an effect is even considered.

Effects require a wide range of support systems: dry ice for example requires special handling and storage; many lighting effects require special power supplies; large projectors will require careful handling. Permission may have to be sought for loudspeaker locations. Insurance is also involved. All these things need to be considered in advance and the implications worked into the production.

Some effects will require additional staff or staff skilled in a particular discipline, this is especially true of pyrotechnics for example. This might involve providing training for the staff in that particular effect. Certainly effects will require additional rehearsal time to that usually allowed.

Backlight

Light which comes back towards the audience and lights the backs of the actors is useful to sharpen up figures and separate them from the background, especially if the costumes are the same colour as the scenery. However backlight can be used almost on its own to suggest darkness whilst enabling the audience to still see some degree of the action. The shadows on the floor can be dramatic and their direction needs to be used creatively.

Back projection

Back projection has a number of advantages over front projection. Firstly in a dramatic context back projection clears the stage in front of the projection beam and thus frees the space for the movement of performers and scenery, whereas in front projection the beam has to be avoided. Back projection enables the projector to be more square on to the screen and thus minimises the kind of distortion which is associated with front projection when the projector has to be at the side of the stage at an angle to the screen. Back projection also creates better access to the projector. (See colour illustration 4). One drawback is that many projectors do not have very wide angle lenses and so the projector could be such a distance from the screen that vital stage space is used up, alternatively the beam can be bounced off a mirror or the picture made up of segments each projected from a separate projector. Back projection screens can be made from any translucent material although the Rosco screen is the most effective; the black screen is totally dark until illuminated by the projection, but many such materials have restricted viewing angles which means that the light level falls off as the image is viewed from the sides.

Bouncing

In the early days of electric light, David Belasco (see page 9) developed the technique of bouncing light off bowed discs so that it would soften and provide a diffused light over the stage. Bouncing light off a surface is standard practice in photography but on stage it has virtually gone out of fashion. However it is useful whenever space is at a premium and the floods lighting skycloths, cycloramas or backings cannot get sufficiently far away to spread properly, instead the instruments should be turned away from their 'target' surface and the light bounced off a nearby reflecting flat, drop or border.

Candles

The first question about this effect is whether real candles are essential to the script as they are in some productions (such as *A Man for All Seasons* where a document is burned from a candle flame). Under these circumstances the local fire officer might permit the use of real candles otherwise their use on stage is rare, however good they might look. There are now several proprietary candle bulbs (powered from mains or battery) which flicker and can look effective from a distance. It is also possible to wrap tissue paper round a low voltage torch bulb and achieve a reasonable effect, albeit without a flicker. (Esquire Jauchem also discusses candles on pages 111–12.)

An important part of the effect is how to replicate the candle light. This involves an analysis of the direction, colour and intensity of the candles in question. Generally the candles will be placed lower than the actors' faces so that the light should ideally travel up towards them giving large shadows on the walls of the set. This can be achieved by hiding small low voltage spotlights in the footlights or in furniture and cross-fading as required. Sometimes these baby spots can be used for a whole scene or at the start of the scene if otherwise they would be too distracting.

Colour

In the context of this book we are talking of colour as an effect and not in its more commonplace use in the spotlights which illuminate actors and scenery. Colour can create dramatic effects and it is wise to experiment first rather than guess as the rig goes up. Small display fittings and offcuts will give some idea even if the nature of the light used is different from that in the spotlight itself and thus the colour might not reach its true value. It was noted earlier that Samoiloff used strong colours to change the colours painted on the backcloth or of the costumes. Certainly a cross-fade from one strong colour, say magenta, to a cool blue, can affect the audiences' mood and this technique is the basis for lighting a production where the changes in the mood of the music need to be supported by lighting changes. For concerts where decorative scenery might be at a minimum, a neutral floor and backing can provide the best foundation on which to project many different colours during the event.

Complex productions requiring a lot of colour changes can thus require large rigs because the deeper the colour then the less light it will transmit. Hence many spotlights are needed to accumulate sufficient light for a deep colour to register. Parcans are the most efficient spotlight in terms of converting electrical energy into light and so these form the key light in rigs

4.1 Semaphore colour change system from CCT.

4.2 Colour change wheel system from CCT.

where colour washes are an essential component. Colour change mechanisms enable the rigs to be smaller and yet still deliver a wide range of effects.

The oldest type of colour changer is perhaps the semaphore which was used on limelights (follow spots) in the nineteenth century. Today's follow spots utilise very much the same system and motorised devices can fit most other spotlights. Usefully on contemporary systems the arms can be placed in the light beam in several combinations thus providing rather more colours. (See illustrations 4.1, 4.2 on page 95.)

Another old type of changer is the wheel which holds five colours (the first one of which is usually white). The drawback to this device is that the colours can only be used in order (the wheel will only revolve in one direction) and thus great care must be taken in the planning. More recent devices rely on a scroll which contains separate colours taped together with heat resistant tape. Sensitive motors move the colours back and forwards with high accuracy so that a single spotlight could offer up to sixteen different colours. Cross-fades can be virtually instantaneous or very slow so that the very act of fading creates an effect in itself – such as sunset. A development of this device is the ColorFader in which three scrolls of colour can be adjusted relative to each other so that a virtually unlimited range of colour can be provided. The manufacturers have programmed the control of this device with the main colour ranges and usually the designer can thus choose any one of 300 or more colours at random. In any device where more than one colour is in the light beam then less light will result and consequently such devices ideally need to be used in substantial numbers to compensate.

All these devices need a power supply separate from that to the spotlight and the scrollers will need a mains supply clean of any voltage reductions and fluctuations caused by other electrical devices on the same line, otherwise older models may have a tendency to slip into colours adjacent to those selected. The nature of the colour medium should be checked with the manufacturer or hire company because many prefer the tougher polycarbonate ranges to be used. All these devices rely on motors and whilst most are relatively quiet this may not be the case if they are all moving at one time, the speed of the change also influences the noise, faster changes being noisier than quiet ones. Additionally most devices incorporate cooling fans which could create noise problems in small auditoria or quiet productions. Changes sometimes need to be linked to loud musical passages.

Different types of spotlights produce different colour effects dependent upon the way that their beams diverge. For example if two different colours are placed side by side in the same colour frame then the profile spotlight will tend to mix them together whilst the fresnel or PC spotlight will project the colours authentically side by side. The profile's beam alters if gobos are placed in the gate and then the lenses adjusted so that the gobo is out of focus, in this case each tiny overlapping projection of the gobo pattern contains the two colours overlapping side by side. Floodlights will also 'project' split colour although the join is likely to be clearly visible on the backcloth or cyc and so some diffusion will be required. (See colour illustration 5)

Fibre optics – stars   These devices depend on the effect of light being refracted along a flexible slender glass tube so that the light emerges at the end of the tube as a tiny, but powerful, dot of light. The most common use for this effect is for stars on backcloths, which are produced from a fibre optic 'harness' containing hundreds of optical fibres all lit from one single light source; a motorised flicker wheel in front of the light causes the stars to twinkle. Since the fibre ends are tiny they can be built into painted skycloths so that a slow cross-fade of the daylight into the stars creates a magical effect. Optical fibres harness for this purpose can often be hired. Other uses include signs and animal eyes in night forests. (See illustration 4.3)

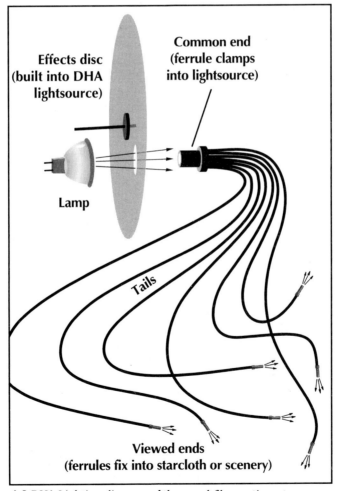

4.3 DHA Lighting diagram of the usual fibre optic system.

Stars can also be projected from a gobo which can be made by hand using a nail, pierce the metal (printer's lithoplate or kitchen baking tin) with tiny holes and use in a profile spotlight which has cleaned lenses sharply focused.

Fireworks

Fireworks can be produced by fibre-optics; LED, neon or other lamp circuits which can be made to chase (see colour illustration 39); projecting composite gobos in quick succession (see colour illustration 40). Alternatively a real 16mm cine image can be projected in loop for repetition. Each option has its advantages and disadvantages, the lamp option is labour intensive to install but would show up in brighter stage lighting than would the gobo or 16mm projection, although these are the more likely to replicate the effect.

Fountains

Assuming that the fountain is not real, which is always possible since most DIY and garden centres supply the components, then it is possible to project fountains by means of composite gobos. The instruments chosen need to have a good balance and locking mechanism otherwise they will not remain in position and the effect will not line up correctly. Several gobos are used (dependant upon the gobo manufacturer and the type of fountain) and each requires a separate dimming circuit which are then chased on an effects panel of the control desk. Some gobos are more stylised than others and this can affect the choice of colour. It is best to back project this effect in order to prevent people passing in front of the beam and in order to get the instruments square to the screen and avoid distortion. Some fibre optics with side emission can also be built into fountain shapes although the minimum radius or curvature is not small and thus they are better kept for larger effects. (See illustration 4.4)

4.4 DHA Lighting composite fountain gobo, static base and three dissolving water effect gobos.

Ghosts

Ghosts and similar abstract moving shapes can also be projected by a spotlight onto a flexible reflective surface such as the tougher kitchen foil which is gently manipulated by hand and directed so that the reflection falls on stage in the appropriate place. The benefit of this effect is that it is totally random. (See also Pepper's Ghost on page 109).

Gobos – projected shapes

The gobo (also called 'pattern' in the USA) is a slide which is inserted into the gate of a profile spotlight which then projects an image of the slide. Although most profile spotlights are fitted with gates, not all are, so it is wise to check the equipment to be used at an early stage. Because the gate of the spotlight is subject to high temperatures the slide must be metal or heat-resistant glass. Gobos can be made by hand using printer's lithoplate or the tougher foil baking and freezer tins. Care is needed to avoid accidents on the sharp edges. Proprietary gobos are available from most manufacturers and the ranges cover windows, trees, clouds, abstract shapes (called 'breakups') which add texture to scenery and floor, symbols and geographic images such as the Eiffel Tower. Gobos can also be made to the customers own design. Several companies have now produced a gobo holder which enables the gobo to be adjusted whilst it is still in the gate. Glass gobos enable more sophisticated shapes to be projected but the gobo itself must be held in a special glass gobo holder and not in a holder for metal gobos. Additionally the spotlight must be tuned so that the beam's distribution is 'flat' or even and not 'peak' which would cause the light, and hence the heat, to be concentrated in the centre of the glass which would then shatter. Spares of the glass gobos are wise. (See colour illustrations 6, 7)

Gobos thrown out of focus produce a multitude of overlapping images which can be used very effectively to suggest the dapples of sunlight or moonlight through trees and if two or more colours are used side by side in the frame then the colours also overlap which adds more texture. Gobos which are required in precise focus are often helped by the addition of a 'do'nut', a metal hand-made mask fitted into the colour frame with a circle cut out to permit the light to pass. This acts like an iris in a camera and can clean up the edges of the image. It also cuts down the light somewhat and experiments with the size of the hole are necessary. Gobos in any event will reduce the light output of the spotlight and thus should be used in more powerful equipment and where other lighting can be reduced so that the effect can register.

Gauze dissolve

This effect relies upon the correct gauze material, sharkstooth or transformation gauze (called 'scrim' in the USA) being used. If lit from the front the gauze appears opaque, once the front light is cross-faded with those lighting a scene behind the gauze, then it (and the painting upon it) will seem to disappear. The lighting of both front and back area needs to be controlled, in front the gauze must be side or top lit predominantly otherwise the light will pass through and light up what must stay hidden. For this to work the gauze must be carefully hung so that wrinkles are eased out. Behind the gauze the light must be contained on the objects, otherwise any which spills back onto the gauze will make it go opaque again. Frequently a black velour drop is hung behind the gauze to prevent light spill and this is flown out just before the dissolve takes place. Several layers of gauze can suggest mists and distance but moiré effects of different fabrics can be distracting. Gauze can also be backlit. (See also **Gauze**, page 15 and **Moiré effect**, page 16.)

Intelligent ('wiggle') lights	Here we are talking of the many fittings which have grown up through the rock and concert market and which provide remote control over any or all of pan, tilt, beam angle, colour, gobo projection and strobing. The more subtle of these devices, such as the Vari★Lite™ luminaire have found their way into straight theatre, opera, ballet and musicals because they can be used in different locations and colours in different scenes and thus reduce the size of the rig as well as providing constant access. However these fittings are commonly used in music events where their ability to move and change provides the effect. It is important to suit the speed, colour intensity and beam width to the music, to establish a translation of what tones in the music mean in these terms rather than to haphazardly move the fittings about. Some of these fittings can only be hired rather than purchased and equally most (but not all) can only be hired with a special control desk and operator.
Lasers	The intense parallel beam of the laser is an effect in itself in that it behaves like no lightbeam on stage, it does not lose intensity or power with distance; its power usually means that it slices through most stage lighting levels and is especially effective through smoke and vapour. However it is the laser beam's ability to be directed that gives the device sophistication. Disco revellers will be familiar with the geometric shapes which can be created but the laser beam can also write messages and draw shapes in 3D, many offer a wide variety of colours. Developments have removed the trailing line of light between individual letters or shapes (known as the 'hidden line') so that each shape or letter has its own integrity. Lasers can now be linked with control devices using MIDI or SMPTE time code so that a degree of synchronisation is possible with other effects and music tracks.
	Lasers are subject to strict regulation because the more powerful ones can damage eye tissue and thus the regulations require that Class 1 devices are firmly mounted at a clear headroom above the audience and performers, and that any reflective surfaces are equally firmly fixed and do not permit the beam to be diverted within a specific range of the audience and performers. Further information can be obtained in the UK from the Health and Safety Executive and the European standard is enshrined in code no. EN 60825.
	In view of the laser's 'high-tech' style they would obviously suit some productions more than others.
Holograms	Holograms are, in theory, an excellent way of producing a three-dimensional effect on stage on an apparent two-dimensional object. In reality holograms are rarely used, the required film is limited in size, the hologram needs to be lit very carefully (not necessarily by a laser) and the viewing angle of many holograms has to be carefully controlled for the effect to retain its integrity. Nevertheless the idea is well worth exploring, especially for small venues, and the increasing use of holograms in security and medicine means that developments are always taking place. This

subject is complex and further reading is advised (see bibliography).

Three-dimensional moving objects have been simulated on stage through the combined techniques of projecting a film of the object in motion onto a three-dimensional model. Perhaps the most notable example of this was the recreation (in large scale) of Lord Olivier's head in the musical *Time* but even smaller and lower cost operations can still produce excellent results. The author recalls an animated 'Father Christmas' in a department store display where the single projection of the face came from a Super 8 projector concealed in the sleigh's lantern!

Light curtain

This refers to a piece of equipment which has become synonymous with the effect made popular by Josef Svoboda who sprayed oil and water into the air and then passed low voltage light through it so that the light refracted and formed semi-opaque walls. Today this could be achieved with cracked oil and smoke (see page 130) but the light curtain is a proprietary device with a tightly packed pattern of low voltage beamlights which produce an intense ray of light. These are frequently used for their intense projection of light as much for a curtain effect and more recent models can be motorised to move the beam across the stage and also to change the colours. (See colour illustration 8)

Lightning

This effect should not be used on its own but linked with the other associated effects of the storm, perhaps rain, real or projected, the darkening of the sky and thunder and rain sound effect (see pages 120–4). Sheet lightning could easily be produced by flickering working lights, floodlights or battens ('borderlights' or 'strips' in the USA), some special photoflash equipment can be hired. It is important not to overuse the effect or to keep the light illuminated for too long otherwise the flood of the beam will cause the audience to witness more than they should. Some floods can be fitted with barndoors to prevent undue spill or proprietary material 'blackwrap' fitted to cut off unwanted light. Forked lightning gobos can be effective in powerful profile spotlights and it is wise to use more than one. However the best forked lightning is made from the use of stroboscopic sources which are faster than incandescent, many of which can accept gobos. Proprietary lighting units like this can be hired out but care needs to be taken with power supplies. (See also page 121)

Linnebach – shadow projection

This effect takes its name from Adolf Linnebach who developed the basis for the modern use of shadow projection and who gave his name to a light specially modified for this purpose. Shadow performances were originally developed by the Chinese but in this application the projection is a still slide to add some texture or suggestion of location onto the backcloth. There is no lens and thus the slide cannot be clearly focused. However this type of projection is the only one in which the slide can be made up in situ and the effect judged. (See illustration 4.5 on page 102) (See also **Overhead projection**, page 105.)

4.5 The Linnebach lantern (on the left) throws a suggestion of shapes on the back wall of a small theatre.

Mirror ball

This device is a ball which is covered with small squares of mirror. It is suspended in the auditorium and revolved. When lit the mirrors reflect the light creating a shimmering effect on all surfaces which can be quite magical. Whilst there are proprietary mirror balls of varying diameters for different sized auditoria, mirror balls can be made by hand using any large football and small self-adhesive mirror tiles. The key to the effect is the light which hits the mirror. Because light travels in straight lines it is important that if the reflected light is to hit the audience that the originating spotlight is placed in the same location as the audience. Several spotlights would be required and each should be as powerful and have as narrow a beam angle as possible. Some fixed pencil beam disco equipment is also useful (because of their concentrated narrow-beam) and follow spots can also be used. The device should not remain in use for long periods otherwise the impact will be diminished.

Moon

The best moon effect is still based on that developed by the Victorians, namely a box with lights inside and hung behind the backcloth. The box should be fitted with some translucent material, such as heavy diffusion filter, to even out the effect of the individual bulbs and also fitted with an opaque mask shaped to represent the appropriate quarter of the moon. In Victorian times the moon box also moved across the night sky and this could easily be achieved today, but three flying lines are needed to prevent the moon box from swinging. The effect is visible behind most backcloths which add a distancing haze to the effect. Moons can also be projected by profile spotlights but, unless back-projected (in which case the light source would be seen through the screen) the shape would inevitably be distorted. (See also pages 124–5)

Movie projection

As with all projection the larger the slide then the clearer and brighter the image will be. Thus 16mm projection is better than 8mm, 35mm better again, and so on. However using 35mm ciné projection and above on a regular basis carries especially strict regulations concerning the projection room construction and this would put the use of this device out of the reach of most productions, unless a projection room already existed. Because 16mm and 8mm do not carry the same regulations, they can be used more freely. There is however a limit to the size of picture which each will project without graininess or undue loss of light. It is possible to hire television projectors (of which the Barco is perhaps the most well known) and most do not have to be a predetermined distance from the screen. It should be noted that only the biggest television projectors would compete in intensity with 35mm and high powered 16mm ciné. The choice is likely to be influenced by the ability of the production to make the film or videotape, the latter perhaps being easier with the advent of home systems.

Moving effects

Moving effects are usually associated with the projection of rain, snow, flames and clouds. Additionally the effect of a passing train is sometimes required. The key decision is to judge the degree of realism required and to keep in mind the support which could be offered from other aspects of the production, sound effects especially.

Proprietary equipment can be hired for most of the effects which will be needed. The effect itself being incorporated onto a loop of film or glass wheel. This is then motor driven in a projector. Most effects are more successful if several projectors are used, driven at different speeds and the beams overlapped. Some projectors have a better range of lenses than others and this should be checked in advance if an unusual, or large coverage of the effect is required, especially when the throw cannot be equally large (see also page 106). It is advisable to check the projector (notably the speed) whilst the projector is at ground level rather than up in the rig. More recently animation wheels have been produced which offer a lower cost method of projecting similar effects to those on the glass wheels or loops. The animation wheel is simply a large gobo which is motor driven and which fits into the colour runners of the spotlight. It is used with a still gobo in the spotlight's gate. A range of wheels is suggested by the

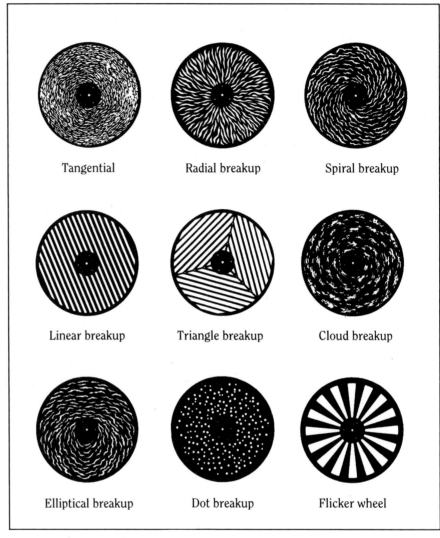

Tangential   Radial breakup   Spiral breakup

Linear breakup   Triangle breakup   Cloud breakup

Elliptical breakup   Dot breakup   Flicker wheel

4.6 DHA Lighting animation discs which work in conjunction with gobos to produce a sense of movement.

manufacturers to work with the appropriate gobo. (See illustration 4.6 and colour illustrations 9–16)

Even cheaper, a simple water ripple effect can be created by placing mirror and other reflective material in a tray of water and causing the water to ripple (perhaps by a can of water suspended above and punctured with a small hole). If a spotlight is aimed into the water then the effect can be projected onto adjacent scenery. Flames can be projected by moving hands in front of a spotlight, in which a variety of 'fire light' colours have been placed, sometimes a flag is used as an alternative to hands. Firelight can also be realistically produced through the lighting control system's flicker repertoire if several different spotlights are connected in different fire colours. Again smoke and sound would be needed to support the effect.

Overhead projection

Although more suited to the lecture theatre than to the live theatre overhead projection can nevertheless be successfully used on stage. There is a limit to the distance which the projector can be positioned away from a screen and still remain in focus because of the nature of its optical system, and the larger the picture then the dimmer it will be. However the overhead projector can be concealed behind scenery and project small images quite satisfactory, additionally since it can be fitted with a continuous roller, moving effects can also be used. Finally overhead projection is also available with Liquid Crystal Display (LCD) screens connected to computer graphic or word processing programs which further extends the possibilities. As with all types of projection, the screen area needs to be kept clear of other light. (See colour illustration 17)

Practical light fittings

Departmentally these are the province of the set designer and he or she should choose them, the props department are usually responsible for their acquisition and the lighting department responsible for any electrical connections. Whilst some period fittings could be made, most will be hired from one of the many companies specially established for this work. It is worth noting that period stage lighting equipment can also be hired. All these items will require insurance and careful handling and storage. Practical light fittings on the set can distract the audience's eye if they are used at too strong an intensity, but, conversely, some brilliant effects can be created if the actual light source cannot be seen but the fitting is actually set at an intensity which produces sufficient light so that the stage lights are only in support of the effect, rather than the prime illumination.

Remote control

A typical use of remote control is the remote dimming of some light fitting on stage which cannot have a lead connected to it and run off-stage to conventional dimmers. In these cases small dimmers can be built into the fitting and operated via a radio remote control system similar to those for small boats and planes. Radio remote control can also be used to trigger strobes, set off motors and steer models. Later in the book Esquire Jauchem also describes the use of photoelectric cells to switch off battery powered candles which are inaccessible in a fade to blackout, see page 112. (See colour illustration 18)

Scenery, lighting of

The matter of lighting scenery perhaps more properly belongs in the many excellent books on stage lighting but some general words might prove useful nevertheless. Firstly it is a wise lighting designer who recognises that most set designers know how their scenery needs to look, but here is a distinction between what the set designer wants to see and how the lighting designer might achieve that look. For example, painted canvas drops which have been rolled up for a long time would traditionally have battens or borderlights at their top edge lighting down them. However this only serves to reveal the creases and so it is far better to light such drops from the front using softly diffused pars or fresnels; soft focused 'break up' gobos in colours complimentary to the set also work very well. Any set which contains a great deal of colour would generally not require an equal amount of colour in the lighting rig, certainly not if the set was highly painted. Conversely if the set was muted in colour, or even white, the designer might have chosen that as a background on which lighting could play in order to change mood and location. Again productions such as pantomimes, rock concerts and some musicals would contain the kind of scenery which is designed to change colour through the use of lighting, as an effect in itself rather than as an accident! (See **Samoiloff**, page 9). Any texture present in the set should be enhanced by skimming light along its surface and the direction which the light (and consequent shadows) take is often a clue as to the direction of the motivating light for the scene, that is sun, moon and so on. Shadows caused on the set through lighting in this way should follow the angle of any painted highlights and shadows. The set designers model should not be viewed as a cute piece of three-dimensional art but as a working tool and the wise lighting designer should use it and experiment with angles of light and colours through small display fittings or torches, such occasions are valuable if attended by the set designer and director. (See colour illustration 19)

Searchlights

What is usually required in this case is the effect of beams of light moving up into the 'night sky' in search of enemy aircraft or heightening some occasion in a similar manner to the popular movie concept of a Hollywood premiere. It is important to find out if the actual searchlights themselves need to be visible to the audience in which case only a real searchlight will do and they can be hired. The effect of the beam however can be replicated through the use of narrow beam angle parcans or theatre lighting beamlights, some of which are low voltage; smoke or cracked oil (see page 130) will help. If real searchlights are used outdoors it is vital that contact is made with Air Traffic Control and with the Police who will be fielding enquiries from a puzzled public ignorant of the event.

Signs

By far the simplest method of achieving a real sign is to make a real sign box, cut out the letters on the face and fill the space with appropriately coloured filter, and fit a light source into the box itself. If the budget permits a real neon or cold-cathode sign to be made, the effect on stage can be stunning. Alternatively a gobo of the wording could be made (proprietary ones cover the usual words 'Bar', 'Restaurant', etc). Fibre optics can also be used (see page 97).

Slide projection

Slide projection is generally used either to represent scenery or to illustrate some aspect of the production through pictures or text. Slides are also used in opera to project translations of the libretto, these are known as surtitles because they are usually projected above the proscenium, one line being cross-faded into the other. The cueing of surtitles is complex and must be done by a person who is competent in both the language being performed and that being projected, in addition to that of the operator of the projectors. Care is needed in order to ensure that the text is large enough for it to be read from the distant seats and this can mean a compromise between the amount of text projected at one time, the rate of cross-fade to the next slide, and the translation itself.

The main aims in slide projection are to avoid distortion and to project a bright, clear and even image. The first can be avoided by mounting the projector as close to the centre-line of the screen, or using special pre-distorted slides (some 35mm projectors will accept lenses to correct keystone distortion). The second relates to the size of the slide and the power of the lamp behind it. Basically the bigger the slide the better the picture. Colourful and detailed slides will absorb more light than clear, simple or monochromatic ones. As with all projection, slide projection relies additionally on controlling other light sources so that they do not spill over onto the projected surface and wash out the projections. This in turn means that the projections must be planned when the set design is being discussed, additionally to ensure that the projectors can be accommodated in the most suitable locations. (See illustration 4.7 and colour illustration 20)

4.7 Rear projection from Kodak Carousels at the Questors Theatre in London.

Smoke, lighting of	The use of smoke and cracked oil is covered extensively in Chapter Five, but perhaps a few words on the lighting of smoke would be useful. Firstly the smoke must be present at all the occasions when the lighting is set, plotted and rehearsed and as is mentioned later this also means that the relevant air handling plants must be on. This is especially important if the smoke is to carry any projections from conventional slide equipment, gobos or lasers; and this is a very spectacular effect. Do not forget that the smoke will soak up a lot of light and thus as the smoke clears the overall stage intensity will increase and might have to be adjusted.
Strobes	The stroboscopic effect is usually used to either confuse the audience or in conjunction with carefully controlled movement by the performers to suggest the flicker of the early moving pictures. Because this effect is very dramatic its use should be carefully controlled otherwise the audience will tire of it and turn away. There are strict regulation governing the use of strobes and they also require notices to be posted to warn the public. The effect can either be delivered from proprietary devices (several of which can be 'slaved' together) or via the effects panel of lighting desks although the response time of incandescent bulbs is not as fast as that of purpose-made strobes. Proprietary devices usually come uncoloured and the addition of colour can alter the nature of the effect, softening it somewhat. The effect works best when the stage lighting is dimmed or faded out.
Sunset and sunrise	Different locations around the world have different sunsets and so it is important to find out sunset times for the location of the production and not 'project' onto the production your ideal design. For example the nearer to the Equator the shorter the sunset is. Additionally, the location of the setting sun will determine the position on stage from which the actors are going to be lit for the rest of the scene, assuming that practicals are not switched on or the moon comes up sooner than normal! This means that the location of the setting sun determines the location of the keylight for the scene. Consequently the sun rarely sets at the rear of the stage but at the side, moving round to the rear at the end of the scene. Sunrise is the same as sunset but in reverse, except that the lower air temperature and pollution can restrict the quantity and duration of the pinker colours. Gobos with split colours are useful.
Tinkerbell	There is a view that the fairy in *Peter Pan* is best left to the imagination of the audience but it is possible to project a dot of light which will suffice. These days low powered lasers have been used for this effect, or the kind of light-pointer which is found in lecture theatres or again intelligent 'wiggle' lights. However it is also possible to focus an iris down a narrow beam angle profile onto a small mirror which is in turn mounted onto a piece of rubber, flicking the rubber causes the reflected dot to move in random shapes. The assembly can be mounted in the prompt corner, fly floor, control room, any where which offers a view of the stage. This is believed to have been invented

by Eddie Biddle, the UK doyen of mechanical effects designers, in response to his employer's request for a high-tech Tinkerbell!

Ultraviolet

This effect is mostly associated, in the UK at least, with puppetry and pantomime when an object or objects are usually moved in a balletic or comic fashion in otherwise total darkness. The objects in question must be painted in ultraviolet paint (see page 15), and a range of colours is available, no light other than the UV should be on at the time of the effect. Some fabrics can also fluoresce naturally and others can do so when washed in most domestic detergent. Thus a check of furnishings on the set needs to be made in advance, and operators of the effects should be dressed entirely in black, including the head. UV equipment is available in fluorescent tubes which are easy to hide and operate instantaneously; older UV floods require time to come to full power. The effect can damage the eyes of operators and should not be used for long periods. UV filters are available for follow spots and can be used in powerful stage instruments but they are not as effective as proprietary UV equipment. Some more recently developed UV equipment in the USA can be used in conjunction with stage lighting. Ultraviolet is occasionally known as blacklight.

Waterfalls

Assuming that the waterfall effect is not delivered through the use of real water (which has happened on stage in spectacular revues and Victorian melodramas) then some use of lighting will be required. (For the use of real water see pages 30 and 123.) Esquire Jauchem staged a brilliant waterfall effect for a production of *Der Freischutz* which I lit in Boston. Dry ice fog was passed over a translucent waterfall structure. Several water effects projectors underneath the structure provided added movement and enabled the light level of the effect to be precisely controlled.

ENDPIECE

The best collection of effects I have ever seen was created by Esquire Jauchem, Herbert Senn and Helen Pond for the production of *Der Freischutz*. The central theme of this short scene is that the hunter must attend the Devil's Gorge at midnight to receive his seven magic bullets which will be forged by the Devil's Henchman. A ghost must appear each time a bullet is forged and other events also occur. The ghosts were created by using an enormous Pepper's Ghost system. A large plastic sheet was suspended at an angle mid-stage, the figures representing the ghosts were placed behind a rock and lit from a battery of par lamps to create sufficient intensity which reflected up into the plastic. In the early rehearsals the wind movement caused by the ghosts getting into place was sufficient to cause the plastic to ripple and thus to cause the reflected image to dissemble and then assemble once the ghost had got into place and was stationary. This was a stunning effect in itself and one of those happy accidents which take place on stage. The ghosts had to appear in a waterfall which was built as descibed above. Among the other effects were fibre-optics representing eyes of animals in the forest and built into the trees; a large snowbag effect filled with dried beans to represent hail; bags of leaves blown around the stage by large fans; a meteor crossing the sky; a lighting bolt; batteries of xenon lightning projectors; and flame projectors onto the trees. Esquire has described many of these effects in the next chapter.

My favourite effect came from the representation of steam as the 'hot' bullet was placed into cold water to help it solidify, the steam came from a CO_2 cylinder operated by a technician built into the rock on which the action was taking place. The tubing connecting the cylinder to the bucket was so long that the 'steam' had to be sent precisely on cue otherwise it would not emerge in synchronisation with the 'hot' bullet. Thankfully the music provided a good base and the cue was never missed.

The above is an example of a scene which depended upon effects and worked, but early in my career as a lighting designer I provided an example of how not to do it. The occasion was when I was lighting a production of *Night of the Iguana* at RADA, and since this was the first show I had lit here I wanted to demonstrate what I could do. So for the storm sequence I hired fleecy and storm cloud projectors, rain projectors, lightning effect projectors and additional floodlights so that I could achieve a great variety of sombre colours on the wraparound cyc. Douglas Heap's set had provided an ideal canvas with a small collection of louvred doors in the hotel at one side through which it was possible to throw good patterns of light as the guests retired to their rooms. There was a scrubland built towards the back of the stage, some real trees and telegraph poles. Each was carefully lit with gobos and as the storm started the light blue sky slowly changed to dark blue and then to deep purple with a hint of green. The fleecy clouds gave way to storm clouds and gobos and louvred patterns filled the rest of the stage; as it got increasingly darker the rain, thunder and lightning all started. It looked fantastic. But I found out that some members of the audience were coming back to extra performances just for the storm scene and then going home again. I had distracted them totally from the play.

More recently a beautifully simple effect was created by Michael Spencer in his design for *Macbeth* for Welsh National Opera which I lit. Michael conceived a totally black box which would truck up and downstage and swallow up everything in its path (such as dead bodies) and then move back upstage and reveal that they had disappeared into the black hole. Conversely the black box would truck upstage and the witches would appear out of the darkness. Like all the best ideas it is simple and was terribly effective. From my point of view the idea required crosslighting and virtually no front light so that the blackness of the box was always maintained and characters would be crisply lit against the darkness. Recognising this Michael had provided clear wings in which to place equipment. A good example of a designer who knows how light works. (See colour illustration 21)

5 Special Effects

ESQUIRE JAUCHEM

FIRE

One of the trickiest challenges designers routinely get thrown at them is representing fire on stage – from the simple act of lighting a candle to burning an entire city night after night. Two questions need to be addressed immediately: how realistic does the fire need to be and what are the local fire codes governing the use of real flames.

Basically the elements necessarily present to create the illusion of fire if real flames are impractical or illegal are smoke and flickering or moving coloured light. Note here that real fire is not red. Light a match and look at the flame, yellow is really the predominate colour in most fires. Glowing embers tend towards orange/red and oxygen rich fire can be bright blue. On stage, I find that a yellow/orange tends to read as realistic fire in most circumstances with other colours mixed in for texture.

Candlelight

Let's start simple – suppose we need a candle to be carried on and placed centre stage on a table in a realistic drama. Easy enough, just get a sturdy candlestick and go for it. But, we are in a town that allows no open flame on stage. That simple candle just became a major project that costs money and requires some expertise in electronics and prop building! Most off-the-shelf electric candles look pretty stupid on stage. The monotonous glow of a battery powered bulb could well get a snicker from your audience and be annoyingly distracting at best.

A Swedish company solved this problem by creating candles for churches which had a very realistic flame-shaped, plastic covered bulb which is mounted on small springs so it actually moved when the candle is carried or air is passed over it. These candles were very fragile but quite effective. Electric candles have one major drawback: you can not do a blackout on stage because your candles will just flame on!

This can be solved if an actor is nearby and can turn it off . . . but with your luck every character on stage is either asleep or dead. A miniature, photo-electric cell controlling a switch in the candle circuitry can be mounted on your candlestick where the overhead lights will shine on it. When the stage lights go out, the cell will sense the change and trigger the switch, and your candle will go out. You will need a sensitivity control to adjust the level of light necessary to keep the candle circuit activated.

Another effective imitation candle has been achieved mounting several small, bright 'grain of wheat' incandescent lamps in a plastic flame shape and causing them to have a random electronic flicker. One constant lamp in the cluster keeps the effect from being too 'flashy'. They can be battery powered or hard-wired. This type of candle is available commercially from special effects companies (see Appendix A, page 141) and was used to create the massive candlelit scene in *Phantom of the Opera*.

Torches

If real fire is allowed this is fairly easy. A juggler's torch which is doused with lighter fluid or odourless charcoal lighter fluid can be very impressive. One can dance, juggle, run around and generally carry on like a savage to great effect. Your costume and set designer must be warned to avoid anything gauzy or flammable. Wigs and headdresses can also be of particular danger. You must always work with the performers to make sure they understand the dangers involved. The biggest problem with this type of torch occurs when the chorus of 50 rebels carrying 20 torches runs into the cramped wings and the torches keep flaming away lighting up stage hands and stored scenery, not to mention a frightened diva about to make her big entrance. Stragetically placed buckets of sand can be helpful up to a point as well as stage hands with wet towels to douse the firebrands, but in sufficient numbers one can have a real problem of logistics.

Enter the butane torch, gas powered, adjustable flame size, with a lever that, when released, kills the flame instantly. These very spectacular units are much safer and can produce even larger flames. They are more popular with fire departments since they self-extinguish if dropped on stage and can be turned off as actors head into the wings. They were used in the original production of *Evita* and have been popular in theatre and opera ever since. (See illustration 5.1 opposite)

If real fire is not allowed on your stage, you are quite frankly, out of luck. I have made several, and seen many, artificial stage torches, and I have yet to see a truly effective electric version. Twinkling lights, little fans with motors and silk or cellophane, mylar etc. They all have limited effectiveness unless you are performing in a stadium and no one is closer than 33 feet (10

5.1 Gregory Meeh holds a butane gas powered torch.

metres) from the stage. About the best one can do inexpensively is to get a massive flashlight (the industrial type with about six batteries in a row down the handle) with a mass of crumpled, twisted gel on top. You need the multiple batteries to get an intensity bright enough to read on stage and the unit is already the right shape for a torch, ready to be decorated to suit your production style. A few silver sequins or bits of mylar glued into the gel will read like sparks from a distance. It is worth the investment in rechargeable batteries if you use the torches extensively or you are headed into a long run.

As with any fire effect, the general light levels need to be kept low when candles or torches are used to get the best visual impact.

LED's (Light Emitting Diodes) which glow bright red and use very little power can be mounted on a stick and battery powered to imitate the glow of an ember. They are even more effective if they can be made to blink and chase. LED's also come in a variety of other colors and can be useful as small, bright points of light (see colour illustration 37).

Fireplaces

A common request that can be very annoying if not handled effectively. If real fire is an option, there are commercially available gas-powered units with cement logs and remote controlled igniters that can be run on propane or compressed natural gas (CNG) from backstage and work just fine. Make sure your set is properly fireproofed and that you have provided to exhaust the fumes safely. These units are expensive to buy, they can be rented from effects and prop companies. The best commercial electric fireplace effects involve a rotating drum with cutouts and lamps arranged inside concealed behind an arrangement of logs. Eventually the repetition of movement in this type of unit can be detected. The techniques described below can be used to build your own very convincing fire.

Camp fire/bonfire

Now we are getting into custom made, fun challenges. Remember, Smoke + Light = Fire, the basic conflagration recipe. Get some smoke coiling up, add some bright lights under it, keep them randomly pulsing and you can produce a very convincing fire up to a couple of metres in diameter. If you have logs, carve holes in them and decorate the grooves with some crumpled red foil to read as hot coals or glowing embers and you are in business. The smoke can come from a fog machine concealed in your prop fire or ducted in from behind or beneath the unit. Some small, quiet muffin fans can help the illusion of heat forcing the smoke up into the air once the fire takes off. Be sure to use flood type lighting instruments to avoid seeing defined beams of light cutting through the smoky air. Fresnels with the lenses removed work quite well as do wide beam par lamps in short cans. Bare lamps can be very effectively built into custom units, but be sure to account for the heat they generate or you can end up with a real fire on your hands!

Fire machines

Since the electric motor was invented, enterprising stage technicians have been blowing fabric up in the air to imitate flames. They were updating a baroque theatre technique of using waving silk to represent the fires of Hell. It usually looks pretty silly and totally fake which can be amusingly appropriate in a stylised production. If realism is the goal, these old war horses can be given some high-tech twists and they become quite convincing. (See colour illustration 22)

When faced with the challenge of burning Beverly Sills, the famous opera diva, at the stake in the final scenes of *Norma* I could obviously not use real fire but the Director, Sarah Caldwell, insisted that great flames should be leaping up around her star! I solved this problem by building a large fire machine 10ft by 16½ft (3m × 5m) which was concealed in the rocks below Miss Sills and on cue, Sarah got her flames jumping 6½ft (2m) into the air to toast the Prima Donna Assoluta. It was convincing enough that during rehearsal, a stage hand caught sight of the flames from the back of the theatre and ran into the lobby yelling for help to put out the fire on stage!

The trick to making this effect realistic lies in the use of extremely thin silk and adding very powerful uplight to make it glow brightly. The fabric must be silk to float properly and it must be very thin in order to get large flames which rise and fall realistically and have a transparent quality. Silk is rated in thickness and I have used what is known as 2.75 'mummy' china silk. It will take some searching to find it (see Appendix A, page 141) and you will usually have to buy an entire bolt of white wholesale and dye it. Remember, use orange dye not red. Don't worry if it is splotchy, in fact it looks better. I even spattered some black dye onto the silk for variety. (See colour illustration 23)

A series of variable speed, 30in (76cm) fans were grouped together and covered over with hardware cloth. By trial and error with the fans running, the silk was cut into large flame shapes just long enough to have sufficient weight that they would rise and fall realistically and not just flap in the breeze. Wear tight fitting goggles to avoid the dust which inevitably gets blown into your face during this process. Note: the fans were mounted in square boxes and it is important to cut a solid cover to place over the fans with a circular hole the same diameter as the fan blades. This will avoid downdrafts in the corners and focus more air into the silk. Be sure to allow space for air to get into the bottom of the units and protect against the silk strips being pulled into the air intakes. It is advisable to cover the inlets with wire or plastic mesh.

Lights were placed under the unit, about 5ft (1.5m) below the fans. The more lights you can manage the more realistic the fire. I had at least 20 parcans with various gels focused through the flames and flickering randomly. Some were constants and other dipped to 50 per cent. Smoke was blown up in front of the unit. If smoke is blown directly onto the silk it will eventually soak into the fabric and make the 'flames' fall down. The result is quite spectacular and limited only by the space you can take up on stage. The fans are noisy due to the volume of air being pushed through so music or other sound effects will be necessary to cover the noise. As with any artificial fire, a scrim in front of the effect is helpful, as are scenic elements like trees, bushes or fences through which we see the fire. Cast members moving in front of the flames and reacting appropriately can aid in confusing the eye and reinforcing the effect. I used this same silk and light technique on film in Maurice Sendak's *Nutcracker* and the results were very realistic (see colour illustration 24).

Disneyland has an impressive variation of this classic using plastic sheets instead of silk for their 'Pirates of the Caribbean' ride. The plastic is secured loosely in window frames with light reflecting up through it. I tested free floating plastic flames but they built up static electricity and stuck together. In windows and similar contained areas, however, it is very convincing.

Firestorms

Several times my associate Greg Meeh and I have been called upon to burn entire cities on stage. First it was Moscow in Prokofief's opera, *War and Peace*; then Carthage in Berlioz's *Les Troyens* – both USA premieres, the Temple of Solomon in *Nabucco*, and most recently, Corinth, in Chereubini's *Medea* (in association with Lighting Designer, Graham Walne).

Large stage fire effects need to be planned carefully in advance in association with the director, lighting designer, and set designer. A few basic principles apply:
1)   keep building the effect, adding new elements;
2)   keep the focus changing so that the audience does not look at one illusion long enough to figure it out and get bored with it;
3)   don't repeat the same effect.

In *Nabucco*, for example, first torches with real flames were seen being carried across the stage. Then, as the fire started, smoke appeared from one are and then another. A huge Menorah set piece flared with propane jets. (See colour illustration 25) Then lights flickered and built in intensity in the smoking areas. Silk fire machines between columns and in doorways shot flames upwards and the light cues built in intensity. Moving fire projections from high-powered Austrian Pani units added to the climax.

In *Medea* we added 16mm xenon projectors with colour film of actual flames shot in slight slow motion. The set was a white Greek temple and the flame projections were truly startling. The fire built to the point where huge 'stones' from the columns fell, accompanied by explosions of flash pots and a huge lintel collapsed as the chorus ran off screaming and Medea rode off in a flaming chariot to join the Sun! The only limitation is your imagination and the budget you have to work with, and very importantly, how much time you have to rehearse to get it all to work.

EXPLOSIONS

The real ones are dangerous, but impressive; the fake ones are safe, but can be ineffective. If you are in a situation where you plan to use pyrotechnics you need to clear your plans with the local fire department and get a qualified pyrotechnician to help you set up your effect. Most towns require a licence to set off explosives and for good reasons, an inexperienced operator can be burned, lose a finger, an eye, or worse; and put the performers at risk if pyrotechnics are not rigged carefully. Regulations also cover how the pyrotechnics are stored. Do not work with pyrotechnics without the proper training and permits.

One of the most important safety rules applies to the triggering of your effect. Pyrotechnics must NEVER be set up to fire automatically. They must be detonated by a technician who has a direct line of sight to the effect. If the individual pushing the button cannot see the effect for any reason (scenery gets in the way, people standing in the line of sight) then they must not fire the effect. The reason for this is fairly obvious, if you cannot see the source of the explosiion, you do not know if it is safe. In all the years I have worked on effects I have only had one accident with an explosion and it can illustrate what I am talking about. In the battle scenes in *War and Peace* in the 6,000 seat outdoor theatre at Wolf Trap Farm Park in Vienna, Virginia (USA) we had many flash pots arranged around the stage to simulate cannonballs landing and exploding. Because the explosions were indicated specifically in the music, and they were numerous, sometimes in rapid succession, with soldiers running around the stage, it was a real challenge. I chose to put the explosives under platforms and ramps so that there was no risk that someone could be standing on top of a pot when it went off in the confusion of the 'battle'.

During one performance there was a loud bang followed by a loud scream. The bang was in the score, the scream was not. I rushed backstage to see what happened and I discovered that a stage hand had crawled under a platform and fallen asleep on a flash pot. His wake up call was loud, hot, and smoky! Luckily, he was more frightened than hurt, although he did get his clothes burned and his skin scorched. It could have been much worse. My operator had a clear view of the stage at all times, but he could not see under the platforms. We should have fenced them off so that no one could be under there. A lesson learned the hard way. With 'pyro', you must assume the worst and prepare for it. Warning signs everywhere, clear explanations of the danger to performers and crew are essential. Don't be pressured by anxious directors, if you have not had time to safely rig the effects and show the cast what is going to happen DO NOT FIRE THE PYRO! You may get hysteric fireworks from your producer, but it is better than a trip to the hospital.

Since the Chinese invented gunpowder, the basics of creating a controlled explosion are relatively unchanged. A powder (usually powdered magnesium known as 'flash powder') is ignited by a fuse (usually electrical) and the rapid combustion produces volumes of smoke, light and heat. In a container with an opening this causes a rapid expulsion of gases out of the opening and you get a jet effect with pressure exerted on the container in the opposite direction of the opening. In a closed container you have a bomb which will burst from the pressures and fly in pieces in every direction. This is very dangerous and powerful, This is what armies throw at each other to kill people. Don't put combustibles in a closed container and ignite them!

A traditional flash pot is made of sturdy metal about 10in (25cm) in diameter and of about equal height. The top is covered with heavy wire mesh to keep items from falling into the box. The flash powder is placed loosely in an open cup at the bottom of the box, an igniter is placed into the powder and the mesh lid is closed. The box must have a cord at least 6ft (2m) long, and once the pot is loaded the cord can be plugged into the firing circuit. Never work on a flash pot that is plugged in. If for any reason the circuit should be hot, it will blow up in your face. Always keep the unplugged end of the cable in sight. It is not enough that you went backstage and unplugged it yourself, if you then start work on the flash pot and some idiot plugs it in, you will get scorched, not him. (See colour illustration 26)

The igniter in the pot can be as simple as a whisker of thin copper wire which heats up and burns when it is shorted, or an 'electric match', or model rocket igniter. Do not used blasting caps, they are quite explosive and can blow a hole in your hand if accidentally fired. Always wear safety glasses (plastic lens), leather gloves and long sleeves when working with any explosive substances. Any electrical wires exposed to the explosion must be made of fire proof materials (ie, glass wrapped insulation). Once the pots are loaded, bright signs should be placed nearby to indicate 'Danger, Active Explosives'. Don't leave these signs out when the pots are not loaded or your cast will get used to them and they will lose their impact.

Due to the dangers involved, it is not recommended that you attempt to build pyrotechnic devices. Rely on commercially available equipment and supplies which have been designed by professionals and which have been tested for safety.

The control box for any pyrotechnics should have a separate circuit for each effect to be operated. Each circuit must have an 'arm' switch which separately controls the power in that circuit. It should be a toggle type, double pole, double throw switch which will kill the power in both sides to show the line, preferably a lighted switch with a bright red indicator to show when the circuit is powered up ('armed'). The actual firing switch in each circuit should be a double pole push button, momentary contact switch, which controls your line. When I build a control box, I also install a locking switch which kills the power to ALL of the circuits and I carry the key to that master switch with me so that no one can arm the controls while I am out working on the effects. (See colour illustration 27)

A protector over the push buttons, so that they cannot be bumped and set off accidently, is also a good idea. Buttons are available with snap covers which must be opened to reveal the switch. Never arm the circuit until just before the effect, and again, don't push that 'fire' button unless you can clearly see the area of the effect and you can see that the performers are safe. Watch for costumes trailing over flash pots, props dropped or thrown on them, or scenic elements like a drop which may flop over your effect as it is flown in. The blast at the source is hot enough to set most fabrics on fire. About two metres away from the heat is diffused and should not cause damage, but it will discolour scenery with the smoke generated.

The amount of powder to use is a matter of trial and error. Start with a small amount and increase the dose until you have the effect you want. You cannot judge a load by volume. A scoop of powder, depending on how loosely packed, can produce very different results. You must measure powder by weighing it with a sensitive scale (powder scales are available at gun shops). Safety measures are even more important when measuring out individual charges from your store of powder, because you can be working with a volume of powder and the potential for a large explosion is present.

Obviously you must not smoke or allow anyone to smoke in the area where you are loading charges. Never make any moves that would grind the powder, these are explosive materials and they can be set off by friction or pressure. Store the material in locked metal cabinets. Measure your charges into small paper packets which are then dumped into your flash pots. The sight of someone nonchalantly dumping flash powder from a full bottle into a unit gives me shudders. Should that unit be triggerd, the whole bottle would explode and cause a major injury. The damage would be much less severe if a small amount in a packet were involved.

For loud explosions use commercial units known as concussion mortars. They are made of heavy steel and confine the charge to produce a loud 'bang'. Be sure your unit is securely fastened to the floor or the set. I have seen flash pots jump several feet when unsecured.

Various substances can be added to the mixture to increase the smoke output or add sparkling effects. Real gun powder adds much more grey smoke and an authentic odour if you are doing period war scenes. Aluminium filings sparkle silver, iron filings sparkle gold, and various chemicals can change the colour of the flash. Commercially available charges come in all sizes and colours. Several manufacturers sell ready-made systems with igniters, cables, controls and pre-measured powder loads. For most purposes it is better to use one of these systems rather than trying to create your own effects from scratch. Many brands of flash powder now come in two parts which must be mixed. They are not explosive until combined. Only prepare what you are planning to use. This formula avoids the strict restrictions on shipping explosives through the mail. Don't ever throw a bottle of flash powder in your suitcase and head for the airport. It can qualify as a bomb and land you in jail.

Set pieces, drops, curtain and anything else in the immediate area must be thoroughly fire proofed. Any items within half a metre of the actual explosion must be totally non-flammable. I usually try to cover anything hit by the blast with tin or aluminium sheeting.

If you cannot use real 'pyro', then you need to create the illusion of your explosion. Again, it is helpful to consider its basic components and then recreate each one to build an artful effect. You need a flash of light, loud noise, flying debris and smoke. The light can be accomplished with a large flashbulb, strobe or even just a par can switched on and off quickly. Sound effects compact discs are now available for just about everything from a fire cracker to an atomic blast. The debris can be Styrofoam (flame-proofed polystyrene) or crumbled cork or any other light substance that will not hurt your talent or audience should a stray piece hit someone. A very helpful piece of equipment is the air canon. It is essentially a metal tube with a compressed air tank at the base. The tube is loaded with your lightweight debris and the air pressure is released on cue throwing the contents into the air. Depending on the weight and quantity of the load you can propel items up to 26 feet (8 metres) into the air. Mixing in some cornstarch will add a dusty look to the exploding pieces. If you cannot find or afford an air canon, you can rig a spring or elastic-powered catapult to achieve a similar effect of firing items into the air or letting them fall from above.

To enhance the effect, your setting should react to the blast. For example, doors and windows can be rigged to fly open or shelves can fall dumping various props to add to the confusion. Pieces of scenery can also be rigged to tilt or tumble appropriately. Smoke has been mentioned previously and should definitely be added to complete the illusion.

ATMOSPHERIC EFFECTS

'When shall we three meet again,
In Thunder, Lightning or in Rain . . .'
Macbeth

Leave it to Shakespeare and just above every other major dramatist or librettist to stir things up, they love stormy weather. Let's break it down to the elements (no pun intended) and see how we can tackle this venture.

Wind

Easy enough, a fan from the local hardware store will serve quite well unless you are on a large stage. Adjustable speed gives you some control. Larger fans are available from industrial equipment suppliers. They are normally rated in CFM (cubic feet per minute) so you can look through a catalogue and go for the biggest punch. Rotary fans with propeller type blades move a lot of air and are fairly quiet unless they are running at very high speeds. Be sure that your fan has a grill protecting both front and back and if there is any chance that the lovely forest drop or the leading ladies wig will be sucked into the fan, add a fine mesh guard over the whole unit.

Centrifugal blowers are good for creating a concentrated air stream and since they pull the air from a small intake, you can duct the air into the fan and avoid the hazards described above. There are a few problems involved in using large fans on stage: they are noisy and they tend to blow around everything in sight. This can be messy if you have scenic drops you are trying to fly in and out. The large amount of moving air can stir up dust that has been idle for centuries and it is guaranteed to blow any fog or smoke effects that you are operating right out of the backstage door.

If you need to do wind and fog or smoke at the same time you are better off placing a few small focused fans strategically around the stage to hit a flag or drapery, or to blow the starlet's golden locks about. They will not wipe out your fog banks and can create the illusion of a wind storm. If you want the fog itself to move, large, low-powered slow fans are required or a vertical row of small 'muffin' fans in a stack. It takes very little air pressure to get your fog swirling, in fact a stage hand in the wings waving a large piece of cardboard is sometimes your best bet!

Lightning

Distant or summer 'heat' lightning can be simulated with standard theatrical instruments focused through windows, trees, or on your background and operated to flicker via your dimmer board. If you cannot get a satisfactory staccato feeling from the board, build a control with a series of push buttons or paddle type micro switches which can be played like a keyboard. Be sure to gel your lightning instruments with colour correction (eg, Rosco gel #60) to give you a blue white electrical light texture. If the storm is meant to be close by, place the lightning units in groups that hit the same area and fire them in sequence so you get the feeling of motion.

Normally the lightning should feel like it originates high and terminates at ground level. In small theatres or for a very localised effect, banks of blue photo flood lamps work very well. They are very bright and are already colour corrected. Since they have small filaments they do not have the afterglow of some larger instruments. They will flicker rapidly with a sharp electrical feel to the light.

Large, old fashioned, medium screw base flashbulbs, although expensive, are very bright and can be useful if you only have a few performances. I have used them to spectacular effect in operas. For a production of Verdi's *Nabucco*, lightning is described at striking the King when he pronounces that he is God. Since there were only four performances, we mounted at least a hundred small flashbulbs in the set behind him and in his crown and costume. When the fateful moment came they chased from top to bottom in sequence and he lit up like a Christmas tree! (See colour illustrations 28, 29) Again, use the blue bulbs (if you can get them) or gel them with colour correction.

Xenon flash units have replaced flashbulbs for most purposes and they make dandy lightning. The key to using xenon is again, having several units placed so that you can fire them in sequence and getting units which are bright enough to punch through with impact. Photographic flash units can be adapted to this purpose. These units are rated in watt/seconds and it would take 500 W/s to be clearly visible on a large stage. The brighter the better with units in the 1000 W/s range delivering considerable punch. The only real drawback to xenon is the cost. To build a large effect which could require 15 instruments would cost thousands. Each lamp head requires a power pack (sometimes self-contained). Because they operate on very high voltage (between the pack and the lamp) the power packs need to be hung close to the lamps. These are generally flood lamps which will splash light all over the stage so you will need to adapt barn doors or top hats to give you some control.

Effects houses have xenon units in theatrical parcans or fresnel configurations. Heavy duty instruments are more suited to the wear and tear of touring and the knock and tumble of theatrical life. Watch out for disco strobes. They tend to be very weak in power output and you really don't want a strobe effect with continuous flashing, you want a controllable unit that packs a wallop! Treat xenon units with respect, don't open the case of a power pack or attempt to wire up a flash unit yourself unless you are very experienced with high voltage and electronics. The pulse to trigger a tube can reach 15,000 volts and the capacitors, even when a unit is turned off, can hold a residual charge that can stop your heart.

Lightning bolts	If you happen to be so lucky as to have a moving light like a Vari∗Lite™, pop in a lightning pattern and go to town flashing bolts wherever you like. Most of us are not that lucky. A pattern in an ellipsoidal will give you a bolt silhouette on a scrim or cyc but you will have the afterglow from the lamp so the effect is limited. I have also used a 35mm slide projector to briefly project a bolt pattern.

Flashbulbs or xenon lamps can be mounted in ellipsoidals and this can provide a very powerful projected image. There are commercial units with powerful xenon lamps available (see appendix). These instruments can be focused on a mid-stage black scrim and still have significant punch. Since the scrim is virtually invisible, the bolt appears to be suspended in midair (see colour illustration 30).

Faced with the daunting task of creating a lightning bolt to strike the stage at the opening of Verdi's *Otello* in a 5,000 seat theatre in the round, Gregory Meeh and I created a 15 metre Plexiglass sculpture which folded down from the roof girders (there was no fly space). In total darkness it exploded in a blaze of light (scores of sequenced flashbulbs) and was cranked back up in a matter of seconds before the audience had regained the use of their retinas! (See colour illustration 31)

Other realistic or stylised bolts can be created in a traditional shadow box with an appropriate shape cut in the front and lights inside. If they are flashed in sequence and the unit is placed behind a scrim, seen through trees etc. It can be startling. A flash pot on the floor under the bolt can give the illusion that the electric charge has struck the earth.

Electric sparks	Occasionally, one is asked to produce an electric spark on stage. This can be accomplished in several ways. A shadow box with a cut-out spark pattern, lit inside by a xenon flash unit (even a small camera flash or bulb) can be very convincing if it can be incorporated into the scenery or props. If it is a laboratory situation you can incorporate a Jacob's Ladder or real spark gap. DANGER – these units involve very high voltages to produce sparks which will bridge space through open air. You can rent these from effects or prop houses. Take care to protect your actors from accidental contact with the metal rods or the sparks. Do not try to build one of these unless you are very familiar with high voltage electrical engineering.

Recently, a very startling technique has been developed known as 'crackling neon'. This involves a glass tube packed with bits of Pyrex glass, filled with gas and sealed with electrodes at each end. When high voltage power is passed through the tube, a spark like arc is formed between the electrodes, but due to the interference of the glass bits inside the tube it dances around and reshapes itself constantly like a huge electric spark.

Neon gas provides the brightest light in a brilliant red-orange colour (see colour illustration 38). Next in brightness is Krypton, with a silver grey or white colour. Argon produces an intriguing lavender, and Xenon, although the weakest in punch, provides a steely electric blue which is clearly visible.

You can have small tubes custom made for a small three figure sum. I have seen large cylinders up to 6½ft (2m) long and 6in (15cm) in diameter. They are very costly to build, but can be rented and the effect is very spectacular.

Plasma globes

If you are trying to create an exciting scientific laboratory scene or need a knockout 'crystal ball', another resource is the plasma globe. You may have seen small versions of these glass spheres in speciality stores. They have an electrode in the centre from which radiates a constant 'electrical storm' bridging to the surface of the globe. If you touch the globe, the 'lightning' gravitates dramatically to your hand.

Plasma globes are available up to 28in (70cm) in diameter. Variations on the design are being created up to 10ft (3m) high in a cylinder form and can produce varying effects from feathers of light to striking lightning patterns in various colours. These fascinating units are quite expensive to purchase, especially in the larger sizes, but they can be rented (see Appendix A, page 142).

Rain

Real water, if it can be used in a controlled and contained design, can be a wonderful addition to a show. Windows with water running down the outside or a rain pipe rigged to fall into a trough which actors walk through as they enter a door are not difficult and look very realistic. This effect can be accomplished with PVC pipe which has been drilled with small holes and powered by a fountain pump which is available from most garden stores. For larger applications, pipe can be strung along hanging pipes alternated with your electrics and connected with a garden hose to cover as much of the stage as necessary. Heavy duty pumps will be needed to power your system. Your biggest problem will be recovering and draining the water to keep it off your stage and out of the audience.

Water is an invasive substance that will creep through the smallest crack or hole and warp a wooden stage faster than you can turn off the faucet. Plastic tarpauling and epoxy resin on a plywood floor will help but, you will have to make gutters and route your water into a drain that is lower than your floor or install a pump to get it up to a drain. As you can imagine, it gets very complicated and very expensive very fast. On Broadway when Jauchem and Meeh FX worked on *Singin' In the Rain* they devised an entire stage floor that raised up and stored vertically against the back wall. Thousand of gallons of water were stored in tanks in the basement so that they could be recycled due to a drought. It was rumoured to have cost hundreds of thousands of dollars and the stage hands still had to come out and mop up leaks between scenes!

Years later, in Budapest, I was treated to the Hungarian version of the same show. I was fascinated to see what they would do with the rain scene. Water poured from iron pipes hung in the flies, splashed into the pit and seemed to be running everywhere. When the curtain came down, an army of chubby matrons squeegee'd the water out the back door into the alley and then mopped and hand dried the floor. There must have been thirty of them – it was a triumph of low tech!

Rain projections which move are available in strip projectors with a continuous mylar band passing behind a lens or a large disc rotating slowly. Xenon Pani projectors have the brightness and quality of lens to make this illusion work on a big stage. (See pages 103–4.)

Snow

The same projected effect slowed down serves for snow. Punched paper (fireproofed) or plastic flakes can be blown or dropped from above. A traditional snow bag is made by creating a canvas sling between two parallel pipes six inches apart. Holes are punched along one side of the sling and as the pipes are raised and lowered, the flakes fall through the holes. For storage, the holes are pulled higher than the snow which has collected in the length of the pipe. There are also blower driven snow units and rotating drums available from effects houses. A new snow effect uses tiny bits of white foam soap suds blown into the air.

Stars

When the rain stops, the stars come out, of course. Tiny Christmas tree lights, strung on a black backdrop are the traditional solution and it still works. It helps if you paint the lamps with some pale blue lamp dip so the stars don't look too yellow, especially when they dim. Make an effort to avoid straight lines of lights which telegraph the construction plan to the audience. A scrim in front of the lights helps add depth and a sense of subtle twinkle. Of course, if you can use several circuits, mix them up and give them a gentle pulse through your dimmers, you can add texture.

If you have a big budget you can go for fibre optics. Thin pieces of light-transmitting fibre sewn into your drop or mounted on hard, black velvet-covered scenic pieces, produce the most realistic starfields currently available. The fibres terminate at a light source which can be gelled with colour correction and you can even put a rotating textured glass disc between the light source and the fibres to make them truly sparkle. (Illustration 5.12)

If all of this is too complex, patterns projected by ellipsoidals or slide projectors can give you a starry feeling. Or you can resort to an old vaudeville trick and punch small holes in a black drop and back it with a pale blue cyc which is brightly lit. For a modern update, use some shredded, silver Mylar behind the drop to put the twinkle in your stars. Simple, but actually extremely effective. It is rumoured that David Belasco used this technique for his highly realistic *Madam Butterfly* on Broadway and he went as far as to hang tiny mirrors, which moved in the air current, behind each hole. The result was gasps from his audiences and some of the most beautiful music Puccini ever wrote just so those stars could slowly appear in the night sky as Cho Cho San waits in vain for that American cad, Pinkerton.

Moons

If you need a moon in the sky like a big pizza pie you can make one fairly easily. A flat round box with lights inside and covered with white muslin or rear projection material will do nicely. Make sure you allow some ventilation for the lamps or your moon can turn into a fiery sun before you get through Act 1. Some texturing with a translucent acrylic paint on the screen can give you a feeling of contour and depth. Diffusion materials round the lamps inside the box will help smooth out the light and avoid hot spots, as will the use of long narrow, frosted tubes.

As in the star drop above, a circular hole is cut in a drop and netted or filled with translucent projection screen (or muslin). Once this is hung, a pale coloured bounce cloth is located behind it. When lit it will give you a good lunar look, especially if it needs to be large. It can rise vertically or set dramatically by raising or lowering the drop. Clouds can pass in front of your moon by tracking a cut drop in front of it or projecting clouds which could also move. For a Robert Wilson production my partner and I were asked to create a crescent moon which slowly tracked across the sky. The solution was a shallow aluminium box faced with white Plexiglass and lit from inside with battery powered lamps. It was rigged to swing on a gentle arc across the dark blue cyc with a scrim in front of it (see colour illustration 32). Of course, a slide projection of a real moon or a pattern in an ellipsoidal can also light up your sky in the simplest productions (see page 102).

Comets and shooting stars

Occasionally you will be faced with celestial events that need to move speedily across the sky. Luckily they usually move in straight lines in a falling direction. If you can rig a thin metal cable you can then build a unit to slide down with a battery powered light. For a production of *La Donna Del Lago*, designed by Ming Cho Lee, we devised a 3ft (1m) long comet filled with bright rapid, random flashing lights powered by a motorcycle battery. The whole unit was covered with tiny mirrors and it was highlighted with small flash bulbs that were fired by an electronic circuit timed to trigger them erratically as it traversed the stage. (See illustration 5.2 on page 126)

Microswitches attached to the comet started it when it was released from its storage position and turned it off when it reached the opposite side of the stage. The sky was filled with fog and a par 36 (very narrow beam) was built in to shine out of the back of the unit to create the impression of a tail trailing behind. It was impressive (and expensive) enough for the staff in the producer's office to ask me to call upstairs each time we tested it so they could come downstairs and watch like kids on the Fourth of July!

The same basic idea can be adapted for most moving astronomical lights. My partner, Gregory Meeh, recently rigged a miniature version of this design for a shooting star in *Crazy for You* on Broadway.

FOG AND SMOKE

Fog and smoke come in a variety of forms and it is important to decide early in the production exactly what you want to accomplish with your vapours. Do you need to obliterate the entire stage, have a few wisps drifting in the sky, a general haze to highlight the beams of light from your instruments, or a dense murk which creeps along the floor? Each requires a different solution and different equipment.

5.2 Esquire Jauchem holds the Comet designed for Ming Cho Lee to be used in *La Donna Del Lago*, Houston Grand Opera.

Glycol fog

For basic fog and smoke we are fortunate that within the last few years, safe and effective fog generators have become widely available. Prior to this, smoke bombs and oil based foggers were in use. They annoyed actors and singers, leaving a slick on the floor that tripped up the dancers and the fog lingered in the air indefinitely.

German opera companies came up with a glycol based formula which was refined by the Rosco company, who received an Academy Award for the innovation. Various companies now market 'fog juice' under numerous brand names. It is processed through pressurised foggers which heat and vaporise the liquid creating a dense white smoke. The most convenient designs contain a small pump to deliver a constant pressure eliminating the necessity of pumping pressure into the unit. (See colour illustration 33)

The best fog machines now have remote controls that operate with a cable or even an infrared, wireless receiver. Remotes with volume controls give you even more flexibility. You can either place the actual fogger where you need the effect (ie inside a building or behind a rock) or the fog can be ducted from backstage via plastic and wire dryer hose to the areas where you need it. Small, 'muffin' fans (used to ventilate electronic equipment) will be needed to push the fog through the hose. By building a box to contain your fogger you can attach several hoses and route the smoke to various areas. The box will help keep excess from drifting around backstage (see colour illustration 34).

Remember that the fog is hot when it comes out so it will tend to rise. Cooling units are available which pass the smoke over crushed dry ice or refridgeration coils, causing the smoke to creep across the floor. As it heats, it will rise in wisps imitating the mist on a lake in the morning. You can make your own cooling device using a large plastic picnic ice chest. Cut a hole in each end and fit in a piece of plastic drain pipe to attach the hoses and use a small fan to pull the fog through the box. Wire mesh will keep the dry ice in the box and out of your hoses. If the ice gets into the hose, the hose may crack.

Whenever fog is called for, get together with your set designer as soon as possible to work out the ducting system. You will need a number of ports if you need to quickly cover a large area. Unless you want to see jets of smoke shooting out, or you have the cover of darkness to fill the stage, it is a good idea to conceal the outlets behind trees, walls, slots in the deck, etc. and add baffles to diffuse the stream of air as it comes out. Even though the newer fog formulas are not oil based, you will still get a slight build up of a slippery film right at the port, so avoid steps and ramps. Be sure that fog outlets in the floor are covered with grills that are sturdy enough to bear whatever weight may roll or rest on them and be sure that the holes of the outlet are smaller than the heels of your costumes. A leading lady with her heel caught in a fog outlet is not a pretty sight.

If your actors or dancers are wearing very small heels, you may have to resort to plastic or metal plates with quarter inch holes drilled in them. Since the holes are so small, the plates will have to be rather extended to give you enough volume. Long narrow panels parallel to the footlights can cover a lot of territory quite effectively. If heel size is not an issue, various commercial metal gratings are available. These fog pockets can also enclose instruments to uplight the smoke to add to your effect. Clear acrylic with holes drilled as mentioned above are useful when uplight is required. Using very narrow beam par pin spots can create an opaque light curtain in the smoke.

If you need clouds in the sky, you will need to duct the fog up higher in the wings and let it drift in at the top of the proscenium.

Once you get the fog on stage you may want to move it around to represent the winds of a storm or the rising smoke of a fire. Strategically placed fans are probably your best solution, but be careful: it doesn't take much airflow to give the illusion of great drafts. I was once asked to have an army surrounded by swirling mists while its leader stood atop a rock with a flag blowing in the wind. Sounds simple, a nice lightweight silk flag and a hefty fan placed in the wings would easily accomplish this. Wrong. The fan promptly blew all of the fog right off the stage.

After trying numerous tricks, we settled on a small powerful fan hidden in a tree near the flag to get it fluttering, and a beefy stage hand with a large card off-stage to get the fog to swirl dramatically. To circulate large areas of smoke or fog you really need large fronts of air gently moving, not powerful fans. A rip roaring storm in a stage illusion has fog moving at an amazingly slow speed, but in the confines of the proscenium it looks dramatically powerful. Large blades at low speeds work the best. Even with this knowledge I still find that I am liable to over prescribe the fans necessary and it always takes some experimentation to get it right.

If you have the luxury of opening a curtain at the top of a very foggy scene you will find that the action of the curtain raising or parting is one of the best methods of getting great dramatic swirls swooping around the stage. Just before the curtain opens, have a crew member load up the leading edge of the curtain with a dense cloud and then dash out before they are seen. Large pieces of scenery moving on stage or even groups of people rushing in can be very effective carriers of misty airs if you pump some fog into their path as they go on stage. It really is a matter of creating a moving sculpture of air currents.

Be sure to take into account the ventilation system in the theatre. More than once I have created great fog effects in rehearsals only to discover one day that the ventilation system was in a passive mode and was not turned on full volume until an audience arrived. The engineer cranked it up and it sucked up every wisp of fog. You may have to negotiate that during certain scenes the system is turned down or even completely off for a few minutes. Make an effort to stabilise the air currents on stage so that you can reproduce the same fog effect each night. Close all of the backstage doors for effects scenes, have your stage manager include this as a cue. One open door can totally change the look on stage. While rehearsing a show with Beverly Sills in Los Angeles I was called to the production desk and Beverly asked why I had fogged up the stage in the middle of the scene. I hadn't, but when she pointed out a distinct haze clearly visible in all of the lights, I investigated. A backstage door had been left open and the smog from the city had infiltrated the entire set!

You may even need to add a downstage scrim to contain the fog in severe situations. Make friends with the facility engineers, because you may also need to have them turn off smoke detectors for certain effects. Some fire inspectors will insist on having an officer on hand if you disable the alarms. Best to deal with these issues early in the game and avoid last minute hassles and turf wars. Also be advised that the addition of an audience will almost inevitably change the air currents. Until you get the system stabilised, it is ideal to be on a headset with the person running the controls so you can make on the spot corrections. This will avoid sparse looking effects due to air currents and, even more important, smoking out the entire scene! As the show runs, someone out front, the board operator or follow spot tech, needs to monitor the fog and communicate backstage if there is a problem. You cannot accurately tell from backstage what an effect looks like to the audience because of the difference in lighting. I have seen multimillion dollar productions where the designers left and within a few weeks the fog effects had fallen apart. The stage manager in the wings thought they looked fine. For long runs it is best to check in periodically or at least get a trusted eye out front.

To clear the air, most of the modern fogs will disperse within a few minutes if you turn the foggers off. Some manufacturers rate their formulas to linger or dissipate more quickly. Even so, you may have to provide for getting rid of the fog quickly. Composers love to follow a rip roaring battle scene with a beautiful ball for the queen. When the smoke of war hangs around in the glittering palaces of peace, you can get a laugh from the gallery and a call from the producer's office. Depending on the ventilating system in the theatre, you may have to add fans in the wings or overhead to exhaust the lingering smoke or move it around. Don't get carried away, you don't need wind machines. A couple of sturdy window fans with various speeds will usually do the trick, but you may have to open backstage doors, open a window or crack the vents in the fly loft to provide an outlet.

Particulate smoke   Unlike the fog mentioned above, real smoke is made up of tiny particles of solid matter which are hanging in the air. This does not dissipate as quickly as glycol fog and very slowly gets homogenised with the existing clear air so that it can linger for as long as a half an hour. This can be an advantage or disadvantage, depending on the desired result.

Commercial flash pots or smoke pots can be fired off to fill the air as needed. Just remember, you will have to exhaust this smoke very thoroughly when your scene is over or it may hover out over the audience for the rest of the show. The smoke in real fires is often black, not grey/white as produced from foggers or flash pots. There is no real safe black smoke to use indoors. Black smoke bombs are sold but they are for exterior use only.

Some manufacturers are producing coloured smokes that are promoted as non-toxic, but quite frankly, due to the chemicals used to create the colours, I would only use these in large, well ventilated spaces. They usually require a pyrotechnic licence and an electric ignition system. (See colour illustration 35)

Commercially available incense can be very helpful in getting some particulate smoke in the air. For a smouldering campfire, for example, some incense may be all that you need. Try to avoid the heavily perfumed brands unless it is appropriate. Real frankincense and myrrh (crystallised resins) which are used in church ceremonies, and are available in church supply stores, are very effective in producing a dense smoke. They are sold with small charcoal discs which are lit with a match (buy the self-igniting style which are impregnated with chemicals to keep them glowing). As the charcoal heats, the resin melts and turns into smoke. These coals get red hot, so provide a suitable container, and they last for about ten minutes. The odour is quite distinctive, but in the case of religious scenes or ceremonies, it can even be an effective addition to the mood.

A traditional theatre trick has been to produce particulate smoke by heating a chemical powder known as ammonium chloride. This is a white powder available at chemical suppliers. Placed in a container on a hot plate or in a ceramic heating coil, it will produce volumes of white smoke, but it also produces some hydrochloric acid and ammonia. The smell is acrid and can be modified by adding some powdered cinnamon to the mix. Be judicious about how long you leave one of these units turned on because they continue to smoke as long as the powder is hot. It can take several minutes to stop the smoke output. This the technique that was used for years to get a haze in the air at concerts so that the beams from the lights would be visible. It must only be employed in large, well ventilated areas. Ammonium chloride is a caustic substance and should be used with extreme caution.

Crackers

In recent years, the effect produced by particulate smoke in the air has been achieved by oil 'crackers'. These rather expensive units break oil (usually mineral oil, but sometimes regular cooking oil) into molecular particles which then blow out in a fine mist. They have become a standard on the rock and roll scene because they create a haze in the air that is perfect for accenting the cones of light from the rig. They are also used in laser installations when it is desirable to see the laser beams shooting through the air.

With any fog or smoke effect, it is essential to work with the lighting designer and make sure that units are included specifically to light the effect. Backlight and sidelight are almost essential on stage to see a fog installation. One cannot rely on the regular scene lights to provide for the effect. I have seen more than one fog cue rendered totally invisible because it was not lit properly and I have seen actors obliterated by smoke because it was flooded with front light.

Dry ice and liquid nitrogen

One of the most dramatic and beautiful stage fog effects is billowy clouds of wispy white 'smoke' pouring across the stage floor, clinging low, kicking up in the feet of dancers, or cascading down a set of stairs. (See colour illustration 36)

For years this has been achieved with dry ice (solid carbon dioxide) plunged into barrels of water backstage. More recently, sophisticated liquid nitrogen foggers have been employed for the same effect.

To accomplish this with dry ice you will need a large tank to hold hot water (usually a 55 gallon metal oil drum). Electric heating elements are inserted into the drum (often water heater rods) and it is filled with water and heated. A wire mesh basket filled with chunks of dry ice is rigged at the top of the drum so that it can be plunged down into the hot water. When the dry ice (which is extremely cold) hits the hot water, it vaporises into a gas carrying water vapour with it.

The resulting fog is voluminous and heavier than air because it is cold and laced with carbon dioxide. If directed into a hose attached to the tank it can be sent out onto the stage floor or wherever the fog effect is needed. A centrifugal blower added to force air into the drum can incease the output and drive the fog through longer hoses to the stage.

Pulling the basket up out of the water will obviously stop the fog production. Most units will not last more than a few minutes at full tilt until the water begins to cool and the ice is expended. You can stretch this time limit somewhat by lifting the basket, waiting, then plunging it back in. This pulsing can even create effective 'waves' on the floor in a small theatre.

To get the most out of your units, get the water as hot as possible and break the ice into pieces the size of golf balls. Take care in handling the ice! It will burn your hands or any exposed skin badly due to the extreme cold. Always use heavy leather or canvas gloves to handle it. When breaking it up, you must wear goggles over your eyes. If a chip were to lodge in your eye, you could be blinded.

The ice can be stored in an insulated cooler for a day or so, but tends to evaporate. It cannot be stored in any sealed container. The carbon dioxide being liberated from the ice will build up pressure and cause the container to burst. It is best to consider getting a fresh supply daily. It takes about 20 pounds to fill most machines and it may take several machines to cover a large stage. It is not unusual for a Broadway show to use more than 100 pounds per show for a big effect. The length of the fog output is determined by how long you can keep the water hot and continue to add more ice.

For large installations or long running shows, sophisticated foggers have been developed which operate on the same principle but use liquid nitrogen instead of solid carbon dioxide. At several hundred degrees below zero nitrogen is a liquid and it is even more dangerous to handle than dry ice and must be stored in special insulated tanks. It can produce exceptional volumes of fog for long periods and with greater control as recently seen on Broadway in *Crazy for You* and *Beauty and the Beast*.

WARNING: Both carbon dioxide and nitrogen gases are heavier than air and can accumulate in a basement or even a depression on the stage. If an actor or stage hand ends up inhaling enough of either of these gases they can become dizzy and, if not revived with fresh air, they could die. Never have someone lie down in fog created with these gases. Also check storage areas for ventilation. Dry ice, even while it is not being used, is giving off carbon dioxide and liquid nitrogen is venting some gas through escape valves on the tanks.

CUEING

In the theatre, a 'cue' is a signal to any one of the various different technical departments to carry out a function which goes towards the making of an 'effect'.

It is perhaps sensible to look at cues and cueing as though they were part of a piece of music. Once you start to play a piece of music, the instructions on the page lead you all the way through it to the end, at which point you may stop. Similar things should occur in a well run performance. Having received the initial instruction to start the performance from the people responsible for seating the audience (generally known as the 'clearance') the sequence by which the performance starts will then be kicked into gear. It is important that the person giving the cues knows the precise reason or time when each particular cue is given. There should be no cue within the currency of the performance which is randomly given.

All cues should be as a result of something else happening and when all these things have finished happening, just as with the piece of music, you may stop. It is not an uncommon thing to hear the deputy stage manager say to the director, for instance, 'when do I give this cue, why is it happening, what is the trigger?' The action resulting from the cue may take place over a greater or lesser period of time. For example, as far as a light cue is concerned, it will be an instruction to raise or lower light levels over a period of time towards a pre-determined finishing point. With this kind of cue, what can be wrong with it in terms of the overall 'effect' is that is can be too early, too late, too fast, too slow, or its 'profile' (the rate of change) can be incorrect, and it is the analytical perception of the people creating this piece of theatre that is required in order for them to correctly judge the lighting cue within the context of the overall effect. There are other effects which, once the cue has been given, will then proceed of their own accord, if for instance one is having some kind of trick effect whereby a bannister or something of that nature may suddenly appear to fall, break or collapse, having pulled or triggered the mechanism, the effect then takes its course.

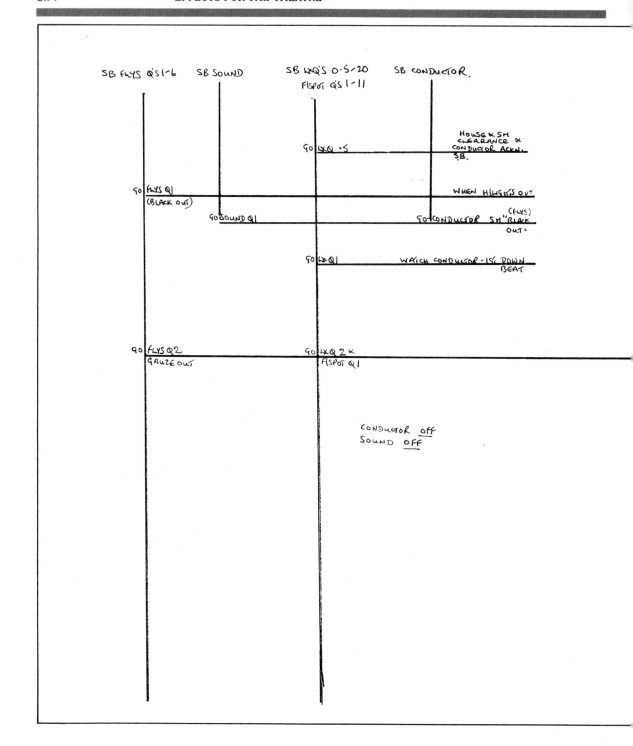

6.1 Prompt copy. The Carousel Waltz. Lyrics by Oscar Hammerstein II. Music by Richard Rodgers. Copyright © 1945 by Williamson Music. Copyright Renewed. Williamson Music owner of publication and allied rights throughout the world. International Copyright Secured. All rights reserved.

Similarly with an electrically detonated puff of smoke, each puff of smoke will behave in its own way in accordance with any local conditions which may at that time prevail, as has been described in the Special Effects Chapter. Sensitivity of cueing becomes essential in order to create the effect as has been proposed by the design team. In the world of the commercial large theatres, the people who are expert in giving cues are highly prized and eagerly sought after by those wishing to put on a show of some complexity.

So in order to proceed with the creation of an overall effect, the stage manager will need to sit down and analyse what various different departments are going to have an input into this overall effect and how many separate instructions might be needed in order for the whole thing to be put together (naturally within sound and lighting a number of different cues may be required to complete an effect). It is then essential to proceed with this envisaged scenario to a point where some kind of ordering of the various different events can be put together. (It must be obvious that in the earlier times when light levels were not as easily controlled and were left largely unaltered, an effect could well be operated by a single department, ie: the scenery department, by effecting some physical change or other in the existing light condition.) Nowadays as we see, the tendency will be for more departments to become involved in this business of creating impact on the audience.

The reproduced page (see illustration 6.1 on pages 134–5) is from a prompt script and indicates the opening sequence of a musical production. You will see that the cues are clearly marked and these are given to the musicians, the lighting people, the sound people and so on, with clear indications as to what should be taking place. For someone operating an effect, and therefore taking the cue, there are equal responsibilities. They must know what they have to do. It is too late, when you have received a cue signal, to try and find out what you need to do. This information has to be memorised, along with the signals you need to watch for to activate the cue. In addition, you need to be aware of the effect the cue has on stage in terms of safety.

Having mentioned the importance of giving cues precisely and the understanding of the cue function, consideration needs to be given as to the methods by which cues are received. The stage management giving the cues will receive cueing information from the lines, moves or the music score in an opera or a musical play. They are then able to mark them as shown on the sample prompt script. The cue should be given by initially 'standing the operator by', and simultaneously putting on a red light which the operator may or may not have to acknowledge. It is at this point that the operator will make a final check of the action to be carried out. On the point of the cue giving both a verbal 'go' and at the same time switching on a green light adjacent to the red light as confirmation of the 'go' instruction. Stage managers are taught to deliver ancillary information first and wait until the precise moment before delivering the instructive or executive word which is 'go'. For example 'Stand by for sound cue 15' (pause) 'sound cue 15 (pause) go'. For the word 'go' to be placed at any other point in the information string would only prove confusing to the operator and may produce messy results. (See colour illustration 41)

The various departments may need to receive the cueing information in a different manner. Some departments are happy to receive simply the light instruction (red and green lights) especially in those productions where there are a relatively small number of functions to perform during the currency of a performance or where verbal communication would be too obtrusive. Others enjoy the receipt of verbal only communications through 'cans' or headsets, because what they are doing is either within a constricted space or it would be inappropriate to have cue lights nearby because they may be seen by the audience. When it comes down to quite specific close work, taps on shoulders, nudges, winks etc, may all be brought into play to effect cueing. Where an individual operator finds it best to take cueing information direct from the action, ie where they may be better placed than the stage management to see the cue signal delivered by the performance, they may do so, and it is known as a 'visual' cue. In this case it is considered good practice for the operator to tell the stage management that this particular cue has been executed. It is an important part of stage management training to analyse the different departments' needs with regard to cueing and to include in the setting up process of the stage, the installation of the requisite verbal and cue light communication systems so that the rehearsals may take place efficiently. The advent of MIDI has led to the development of programmable light cueing systems which use MIDI Show Control protocol in which sequences (usually called 'events') of cues can be recorded and reproduced at the touch of a button as required by the action. Override is possible at any time and operators claim more precision than from manually driven systems on complex productions.

The operation of scenic and mechanical effects is not only a question of training but also of judgment. All scenic, mechanical movement has to be timed and the clear demand for any operator is to have a sense of the time in which the whole function is to take place. For example some directors when choreographing a visual scene-change instruct the stage crew to count in seconds from a common 'go' point and then to begin and complete their action at two predetermined numbers of seconds from the 'go' point. In the world of concert and variety, such signals can be given in terms of bars of music, as in 'tabs in two' means that the tabs shall close whilst two bars of music are being played. Sensitive operators will also understand that the speed of the operation may be varied during the currency of it, that is to say that whilst the draw tabs are shutting slowly, it may look rather better if they are given a sudden impetus to finish off quickly at the end, resulting in a rather satisfactory flick of the drapes as they join up. Lighting controls can replicate the fade profile of a cue and reproduce it at the touch of a button but only a genuinely manually operated fade can match the variations in the timing of the production which makes each performance unique.

Many current productions employ mechanical systems which are linked through to computer controls, where one operator can control the vast galaxy of effects all around the stage. For these to function, great amounts of time have been spent in precisely defining the speeds of each operation and rehearsing them. However, it must be said that already there has appeared comment in the Press as to the rather mechanical effect one gets from mechanically instituted operation. The theatre is, after all, a live art form, performed by live performers, and no-one has yet made a machine which can actually offer the sensitivity of the live operator.

See also cueing sound on pages 47, 60–1.

SAFETY

Not all effects are dangerous; for example in most circumstances sound effects and projected images could hardly be said to be hazardous, although there are safety implications about the equipment used to produce them. It is more likely that other effects such as pyrotechnics and those involving stage machinery would pose a major hazard. Furthermore since effects are not everyday events in the theatre, their production could involve the use of equipment and techniques with which some members of staff are un-familiar. There is inherent danger in this however simple the effect.

This book has contained advice on particular aspects of safety where they apply to particular effects but perhaps the following overview would also prove useful to the reader.

1. First of all, ensure that you are fully acquainted with the regulations governing the premises in which the effect is to be produced. This would assume that you should find out about the conditions of the performing licence of the theatre in which you are working, but additionally, since many performances take place outside traditional venues, in schools and prisons for example, other non-theatrical regulations will govern them and may prevent ordinary theatrical activity in some way.

2. Next make an assessment of the effect involved to see what risk it poses to those producing the effect initially, to those operating it, and to the members of the cast and public in the vicinity. Some countries (notably those in the EU) have safety legislation requiring this assessment to be carried out. The risk is said to be 'high' if harm is certain, 'medium' if harm will result frequently, and 'low' if harm seldom results. High risk items should receive attention first. Re-medial work might involve the provision of protective clothing or storage (for pyrotechnic devices) or re-siting the effect away from cast members, or re-timing the effect so that the operator's view is not obstructed.

3. Ensure that all those involved in the production and operation of the effect are competent. This has been defined in UK safety legislation as someone who; knows the best practice in a given situation, is aware of their limitations, and is able to **take on** new knowledge and experi-

ence. Many codes of practice about the operation of effects are produced by both manufacturers and other organisations (such as the Association of British Theatre Technicians – Abtt), ensure that these are made available to all staff involved.

4. All staff in the EU have a right to training, supervision, protective clothing, environmental protection, physical assistance and recognition of fatigue in their place of work and managements should not rely on staffs' natural tendency to ignore discomfort for the sake of the production. So monitor the production and operation of effects with these aspects in mind and take appropriate remedial action.

5. After each technical rehearsal, hold a short meeting of all staff involved to check if anyone has any problems which require remedial action. Many problems do not become evident until all aspects of the production are knitted together. For example, some mechanical devices which operate perfectly safely in working light could pose a hazard when operated in a lighting cue which was darker than envisaged. Costumes might inhibit the movement of performers who have to operate machinery or props.

6. Provide the effect with the required infrastructure. In pyrotechnics for example this means the use of a proper firing device with lockable keyswitch and test circuit and it is wise to use proprietary devices rather than make one yourself; the same goes for smoke fluid. Ensure that pyrotechnic devices are properly stored, in a wooden lockable cupboard. Provide portable and temporary electrical devices with RCDs (Residual Current Device) which will shut off the power if an electrical fault is detected.

7. If the effect could startle performers, staff or public, ensure that all are aware that the effect is to be operated. This relates to the siting of the device (notably of bomb tanks and the required associated notices), and strobe and lightning projectors.

8. Check the operation of smoke devices to see if they trigger smoke or fire alarms in the building, and also check to see if the building's natural air flow (with all air handling switched on) causes a build-up of smoke in such a way as to obscure staircases or exits. Do not permit smoke to be used on stage when performers are moving close to stairs or the edges of rostra.

9. EU legislation governs exposure to noise levels in the place of work and most outdoor concerts are restricted by their licence as to the sound level they can produce. Elsewhere research has suggested a link between the exposure to high sound levels and hearing loss. All this means that it is wise not to permit sound effects to reach high sound levels for long periods and care should be taken about the level of spot effects such as explosions or thunder.

10. All electrical components should be regularly tested by a competent person. In the UK this involves an electrical test known as Portable Appliance Testing and which covers the devices' insulation resistance

which can deteriorate over a period of time. Visual checks can cover cable and connector damage. Checks on mechanical parts should also be made and one London theatre includes regular X-rays of welded joints of stage machinery. Components should be regularly maintained.

11.   All effects take time to produce and rehearse and it is unwise to assume that they can be assimilated into the production as though they were a normal costume prop or action. If a scene depends on the effects then special rehearsals should be timetabled.

Appendixes

Appendix A
**MANUFACTURERS
AND SUPPLIERS**

Of necessity this list cannot be exhaustive nor can it be accurate through the life of the book, for simplicity suppliers of routine equipment have been excluded, the ones listed below all offer some aspect of effects equipment. If any specialist would like to be included please contact the publishers who will consider additions to the list when the book is reprinted.

Blacklights, Paint

Wildfire Inc, 11250 Playa Court, Culver City, CA 90230–6150, USA
tel 310-398-3831, fax 310-398-1871

Candles

Jauchem & Meeh Inc., 43 Bridge Street, NY, NY 11201, USA
tel 718-875-0140, fax 718-596-8329

China Silk

Horikoshi NY, Inc., 55 West 39th Street, NY, NY 10018, USA
tel 212-354-0133

Colour Changers

Camelont, Unit 2, Cameron House, 12 Castelhaven Road, London NW1 8QW, UK
tel 0171-284-2502, fax 0171-284-2503
(see also Morpheus and Pan Command for the ColorFader unit)

Diffusion Foggers

Reel EFX, 5254 Melrose Ave Ste, 201-D, Los Angeles CA 90038, USA
tel 213-960-4500, fax 213-960-4577
(see also pyrotechnics)

Fibre Optics

MainLight, Po Box 1352, Boxwood Ind Pk, 402 Meco Dr, Wilmington DE 19899, USA
tel 303-998-8017, fax 302-998-8019
Fiber Optic Systems, 2 Railroad Ave, Whitehouse Stn, NJ 08889, USA
tel 201-534-5500, fax 201-534-2272
Par Opti Projects, Unit 9, The Bell Ind Est, Cunnington St, Chiswick Park, London W4 5EP, UK
tel 0181-995-5179, fax 0181-994-1102

Gauzes	JD Macdougall, 4 McGrath Road, London E15 4JP, UK (see also Gerriets)
Gobos	DHA Lighting, 3 Jonathan St, London SE11 5NH, UK tel 0171-582-3600, fax 0171-582-4779 Rosco, 36 Bush Ave, Port Chester NY 10573, USA tel 914-937-5984, fax 914-937-1300 Blanchard Works, Kangley Bridge Road, Sydenham, London SE26 5AQ, UK tel 0181-59-2300, fax 0181-659-3153 (Rosco also supply paints and colour filters) Great American Market, 826 N Cole Ave, Hollywood CA 90038, USA tel 213-461-0200, fax 213-461-4308
Intelligent Lights	Morpheus and Pan Command Morpheus (rental company), 930 Remiliard Court, San Jose, CA 95122, USA tel 408-295-4866, fax 408-287-8178 Pan Command (manufacturing company) 930 Remiliard Court, San Jose, CA 95122, USA tel 408-297-7262, fax 408-287-8178 Samuelson (and Vari∗Lite™), 20-22 Fairway Drive, Greenford, Mddx UB6 8PW, UK tel 0181-575-8888, fax 0181-575-0105
Lasers	Image Engineering, 10 Beacon St, Somerville MA 02143, USA tel 617-661-7938, fax 617-661-9753 Laser Magic, LM House, 2 Church Street, Seaford, East Sussex BN25 1HD, UK tel 01323-890752, fax 01323-898311 LaserPoint Communications, 44/45 Clifton Rd, Cambridge CB1 4FD, UK tel 01223-212331, fax 01223-214085
Machinery	Nobel Elektronik, Box 423, 691 27 Karlskoga, Sweden Hall Stage, The Gate Studios, Stn Rd, Borehamwood, Herts WD6 1DQ, UK Triple E Engineering, B3 Tower Bridge Business Pk, Clements Rd, London SE16 4EF, UK Unusual Rigging, 4 Dalston Gardens, Stanmore, Mddx HA7 1DA, UK tel 0181-206-2733, fax 0181-206-1432
Manufacturers of MIDI Control Programs and Equipment	Richmond Sound Design, 1234 West Sixth Avenue, Vancouver, Canada V6H 1A5 (Stage Manager®, Command/Cue®) Opcode Systems Inc, 3950 Fabian Way, Suite 100, Palo Alto CA 94303, USA (Vision™, Studio Vision™, OMS and MAX™) Matt McKenzie c/o Autograph Sound Recording Ltd, 2 Spring Place, Kentish Town, London NW5, UK email 100014.653@compuserve.com (MIDI Control Program for the PC)
Paint	Brodie and Middleton Ltd, 68 Drury Lane, London WC2B 5SB
Plazma Globes, Crackling Neon	Larry Albright & Assoc., 419 Sunset, Venice, CA 90291, USA tel 310-399-0865, fax 310-392-9222

Projection	AC Lighting, Unit 3, Spearmast Ind Est, Lane End Road, Sands, High Wycombe, Bucks HP12 4JG, UK tel 01494-446000, fax 01494-461024 Optikinetics, Rt 1, Box 355B, Doswell VA 23047, USA tel 804-227-3550, fax 804-227-3585 Optikinetics, 38 Cromwell Road, Luton, Beds LU3 1DN, UK tel 01582-411413, fax 01582-400013 Ludwig Pani, Kandigasse 23, 1-1070 Vienna, Austria tel 43-222-521080, fax 43-222-5264287 Howard Eaton, Winterlands Resting, Oak Hill, Cooksbridge, Lewes, East Sussex BN8 4PR, UK tel 01273-400670, fax 01273-401052 White Light, 57 Filmer Road, London SW6 7JF, UK tel 0171-731-3291, fax 0171-371-0806
Pyrotechnics	Pyrotex Inc, 3335 Keller Springs Road, #104 Carrolton TX 7500, USA tel 214-248-6564, fax 214-380-1770 Le Maitre, 312 Purley Way, Croydon, Surrey CR0 4XJ, UK tel 0181-686-9258, fax 0181-680-3743 Jem Pyrotechnics and Special Effects Company, Vale Road Industrial Estates, Boston Road, Spilsby, Lincs PE23 5HE, UK tel 01790-754052, fax 01790-754051 Jem Smoke Machine Company Vale Road Industrial Estates, Boston Road, Splisby, Lincs PE23 5HE, UK tel 01790-754050, fax 01790-754051 Group One, USA distributors for Jem Pyrotechnics and Jem Smoke Machines, 80 Sea Lane, Farmingdale, NY 11735, USA tel 516-249-3662, fax 516-753-1020
Screens	Gerriets International, 29 Hutchinson Rd, Allentown, NJ 08501, USA tel 609-758-9121, fax 609-758-9596 J412, Tower Bridge Business Sq, Drummond Rd, London SE16 4EF, UK tel 0171-232-2262, fax 0171-237-4916 (see also Rosco)
Sound Effects Libraries	Dimension Sound Effects, 27th Dimension Inc, PO Box 1561, Jupiter, Florida 33468, USA Valentino Inc, 151 West 46th Street, New York NY 110036, USA DIGIFFECTS Sound Effects, Ljudproduktion AB, Lagerlöfsgatan 8-10, 112 60 Stockholm, Sweden *and* Music House (Intl) Ltd, 5 Newburgh St, Soho, London W1V 1LH, UK Stockists of many libraries including BBC, Hollywood Edge & Sound Ideas ASC Ltd, 1 Comet House, Caleva Park, Aldermaston RG7 4QW, UK *and* Gefen Systems, 6261 Variel Avenue – Suite C, Woodland Hills CA 91367, USA
Strobes, Lightning Effects	Diversitronics, 231 Wrightwood, Elemhurst IL 60126, USA tel 708-833-4495, fax 708-833-6355 Jauchem & Meeh Inc., 43 Bridge Street, NY, NY 11201, USA tel 718-875-0140, fax 718-596-8329

Appendix B
USEFUL
ADDRESSES

The Association of British Theatre Technicians (ABTT), 47 Bermondsey Street, London SE1 3XT, UK

ESTA (Entertainment, Services and Technology Association) 875 6th Avenue Suite 2302, New York, NY 10001, USA tel 212-244-1505, fax 212-244-1502

The International MIDI Assocation, 23634 Emelita Street, Woodland Hills, CA 91367, USA

International Organisation of Scenographers, Theatre Architects and Technicians (OISTAT), Lindengracht 93, 1015 KD, Amsterdam, Holland

MCPS Ltd., (Mechanical Copyright Protection Society), 41 Streatham High Road, London SW16 1ER, UK tel 0181-769-4400

PRS Ltd., (Performing Right Society), 29 Berners Street, London W1P 4AA, UK tel 0171-580-5544

PPL (Phonographic Performance Ltd.), 14 Ganton Street, London W1V 1LB, UK tel 0171-437-0311

The Professional Lighting and Sound Association (PLASA), 7 Highlight House, St Leonards Road, Eastbourne, Sussex BN21 3UH, UK

The United States Institute of Theatre Technology, Suite 5a, 10 West 19th Street, New York, NY 10011-4206, USA

Bibliography

Some titles may be out of print but are worth trying to find in libraries and second-hand bookshops.

Aveline, Joe, and Walne, Graham, *Recent Safety Legislation and the Theatre*, available from Book Bazaar, 42 Sydney Street, London SW3 6PS
Baur *Baroque Theatre*, Thames and Hudson
Bond, Daniel *Stage Management*, A & C Black
Collison, David *Stage Sound*, Cassell
Huntingdon, John *Control Systems In Live Entertainment*, Focal Press
Meyer & Mallory *Sound in the Theatre*, Audio Library
Penfold, R. A. *Advanced MIDI User's Guide*, PC Publishing
Reid, Francis *The ABC of Stage Lighting*, A & C Black and Drama Book Publishers
   Designing for the Theatre, A & C Black
   The Stage Lighting Handbook, A & C Black
Rumsey, Francis *Digital Audio Operations*, Focal Press
   MIDI Systems and Control, Focal Press
Rumsey, Francis & McCormick, Tim *Sound and Recording*, Focal Press
Simpson, Robert S. *Effective Audio Visual*, Focal Press
Southern *Changeable Scenery*, Faber & Faber
Thompson, George *Safety in Live Performance*, Focal Press
Walne, Graham *Sound for the Theatre*, A & C Black
Walne, Graham *Projection for the Performing Arts*, Focal Press

Lighting and Sound International published monthly by PLASA (see useful addresses)
Lighting Dimensions 32 West 18th Street, New York, NY 10011, USA
TCI (Theatre Crafts International) 32 West 18th Street, New York, NY 10011, USA
Theatre Design and Technology c/o USITT, 10 West 19th Street, New York, NY 10011, USA
Update published regularly by the Abtt (see useful addresses)

Index